Overcoming Church Hurt Series

Overcoming Church Hurt Series

Biblical Help and Truth for the Hurting

ALL CHURCHED OUT

Vanessa G. Flood

XULON PRESS

Xulon Press
2301 Lucien Way #415
Maitland, FL 32751
407.339.4217
www.xulonpress.com

Many people influenced me to write this series of **Overcoming Church Hurt** *books, but only a few have indeed contributed to my spiritual growth. I could not have done this without their help, support, or blessings. I cannot name everyone who helped to inspire me, but God will bless you for your part.*

I give unforgettable and unwavering thanks to all my family members, but mostly to my inspiring dad, Ronald Flood Sr. (deceased), and my loving mom, Lela Flood. They were always there to pick up the broken pieces, to give me sound advice, and they taught me how to get through life (naturally and spiritually). My mental determination and strength uniquely come from their roles as parents. Mom, you have been an amazingly strong example of holiness, godliness, and faithfulness my entire life, and you always displayed what the unconditional love through Christ should look like. My success is for you!

I would like to thank my animated, funny, and one-of-a-kind siblings, Debbie, Ron, Russell, and Terry; we are a uniquely blessed family and we are "Flood Strong"! Thanks for the children you gave me. I love and appreciate each of you. I also thank my two sisters-in-love Karen and Lashana for being in my life.

I thank God for all my beautiful nieces, nephews, and beloved godchildren. I love each of you, and I cannot wait to see how great you all will be! I pray that you keep trusting, believing, and knowing that obeying Christ is the only way to a better life. Makayla, you will always be my "Apple," and I know you will do great things for God!

Also, I would like to think this book honors the memory of my wonderful Aunts; Juerina (2020) and Ida (2021). I send love to my only living Aunt Hattie and my Uncles, Kenny P. and Top K., and blessings to all my wonderful cousins (especially Charles and Florine) and every relative both near and far!

Indelible and irrevocable thanks to my best sister-friends for several decades, Regina B. and Felecia S. There are not enough words to ever express my love and gratitude towards you and your caring families. Ladies, your laughter, uplifting support, long late-night talks, encouragement, and prayers helped me through life! I cannot thank God for you enough! I love you both (and your mothers) always.

North Carolina
I give an honorable mention to my first spiritual influences and examples growing up in NC (outside of my mother); Bishop C. E. Anderson (deceased), Mother Barbara Ann Anderson, and Mother Patricia A. Loftin, along with the Faith Temple COGIC family from 1978–1998. To my spiritual brother and sister, Pastors Roscoe and Angela Harris, keep going for Christ and living the Abundant Life!

I give great honor and credit where it is genuinely due, and I must say a heartfelt "thank you" to my powerfully anointed, spiritually gifted former pastors, Dr. Carl R. & Michelle Y. Turner, of Faith Soldiers Word Ministries in Charlotte, NC. You taught me how to apply the living word of God to my daily life and how to pray in faith and authority to produce results. I am forever grateful for you both!

I dare not omit any of my sweet friends in Charlotte! Thanks, and blessings to everyone who made me laugh, did ministry with me, ministered to me, worked with me, or blessed me in any way. I love all of my CMPD friends and the FSWM crew (through 2010)! I especially thank Cathy Faye, Shrop, Cheryl "Triple C," Terrell, Shalini, Denise W., SD Jones, and

Aunt Gert for allowing me to invade your loving lives for a season. And to all my former Children's Church children and their parents, you're one of my greatest joys ever!

Texas

A BIG THANK YOU" to Pastor Ron and Pam, and Pastor Tonya; you all came into my life at just the perfect time (Laredo days)! A shout-out of blessings to Texas Southwest (Bishop, Samuel E. Iglehart – 2021), and the Praise Cathedral family and beautiful friends in San Antonio.

Extra thanks to my extraordinary family of friends who showed me so much love: The Watfords (beyond human words), the Banks (a true blessing), the Walkers (always giving), The Deans (Christ-minded), and the Wards (you have no idea). I thank God for my most caring ministry supporters and true sister-friends Cynde W., Pamela Gayle, Kimberly L., Loquetta P., Mother Q., Connie R. and Bridgetta B. May the Lord bless you all a million times over for all your encouragement, talks, prayers, walks, and love. You made me feel so welcome. You extended your family and homes to me.

Pastor Kenneth Wayne & Lady Sallie Davison, I thank God for you! You have indeed been a great spiritual inspiration to me beyond explanation. Your reassurance, love, prayers, and continual faith in me have made a tremendous difference in my life! I love you with the unconditional love of Christ.

To all my loving family of friends, mentees, and fellow Kingdom builders I met at New Life Church, SA ("A Great Place to Be"); I sincerely thank each of you for allowing me to be a part of your lives for a season of beauty beyond the ashes!

There are several others in Georgia (The Jeffreys), Colorado (The Gordons), California (The Ghostons), Memphis (my Sow sisters everywhere), and

Florida (Bent But Not Broken) who have recently befriended me and have been a blessing to my journey. I sincerely thank so many more people for the love, prayers, and encouragement given (you know who you are).

> ***Thanks be to God, who always has caused me to triumph in and with Christ, my Savior. I must continue to bring glory and honor to His Kingdom as I glorify His holy name.*** *I pray His blessings over you all* (2 Corinthians 2:14–15).

The King's servant,
Vanessa

CONTENTS

FOREWORD

By Pastor Kenneth Wayne Davison, Sr.

Firstly, I am thrilled beyond description to render a foreword for my dear sister in Christ! I sincerely thank God for leading Vanessa to take on this assignment to write this much-needed, power-packed, and anointed book. She meticulously deals with the various hurts that people encounter today in churches all over the world.

Secondly, I know of scores of people, including myself, who have been victims of what is known as "church hurt." I recall leaving church many years ago, only to mourn and condemn the actions of church folks who had left me mortally wounded in my spirit. I too, was hurt to my spiritual core after being mistreated by people who should have known better.

There are at least two kinds of people who attend church and become susceptible to "church hurt"; they are those with low spiritual immune systems and those trying to help the sick get well.

I knew that just as people go to the hospital for physical care and medicinal aid, people come to the church for spiritual care and biblical aid. Then, the most fantastic epiphany was later revealed to me by the Holy Spirit concerning that concept. Many come to the hospital for help and assistance but become susceptible to various contagions, such as deadly diseases and life-threatening infections. This understanding is also proper of people coming to the "hospital of the church" for spiritual help. Many who are coming to churches seeking spiritual support get infected by those who are not yet healed! Some get sicker and die spiritually once coming in contact with these highly infectious and sickly people (many of whom are preaching or serving when they should be somewhere healing). Oddly enough, multitudes of people come to the emergency rooms of both hospitals and churches, and they are being mistreated, mishandled, and overly exposed to those who have bad attitudes and septic hearts.

Many essential workers' minds and hands have not been meticulously cleaned or washed before human contact. Thus, causing or spreading all forms of polluted morality, spirituality, and staph infections (which often directly or indirectly come from the *staff*). There is not enough care or training that has been given in many of these help/aid establishments to prevent the ongoing spread of such deadly and poisonous contaminants. Numerous people seeking quality professional/spiritual assistance often leave the building the same way they entered: sick, tired, hurt, cut, wounded, and bleeding.

During my tenure as a pastor, I have encountered scores of people and heard stories wherein people have been severely affected by some church hurt. Many stories regarding their clothing apparel, ethnicity, hair color, makeup preferences, and even their shoes. Numerous others have suffered from some significant church issues. These issues stem from sexual misconduct, shunning, excommunication, position abuse, promotion discrimination, favoritism, nepotism, money manipulation; you name it! All at the hands of a trusted pastor (or their spouse), an elder, a deacon, a minister, and other position holders throughout the church who stalk new members.

There is a way to talk to, deal with, and handle people with love. We must show kindness in the admonition of the Lord; we can do this without killing the spirit and soul of man. We know we are to be cautious and vigilant when driving our cars, cautious and alert around strangers, and extremely cautious with newborn babies. Then why are we not as cautious and vigilant concerning our words, behavior, and attitudes when it comes to the care and treatment of God's people?

The enemy is still busy trying to kill, steal, and destroy God's people. Unfortunately, we see firsthand how he will use the Church and church members to get us discombobulated and weary enough to walk away from our individual and corporate purposes. He wants to take us away from our assignments, distort our focus, and keeps us from the plans that God has for our lives. We must not allow Satan to win against people coming to assemble in the church!

Do not put your trust in what your family says or does not say about you. Do not adhere to the ways of others and their negativity. Do not put your faith in a church building or churchgoers. Do not even put your confidence in a pastor or religious leader (because they should not be your God or your standard of holiness), but put your faith, trust, hope, healing, and recovery in the capable hands of Jesus Christ and the word of God!

When you read this book (and those to come), you will discover Vanessa's arduous plight of navigating through her hurt and perplexing circumstances Despite all the negative issues that she has gone through and has experienced in a church, she did not quit on God or quit connecting, fellowshipping, unifying, and blessing the Christ-established body of believers. Her obedience is remarkable, as she is still looking unto Jesus, the Author and Finisher of her faith! His strength, power, and Spirit are actively working in and through her life in a powerful way!

I pray that this book will teach your heart and mind with the proper posture of servitude, gratitude, and a godly attitude, thus enabling you to receive the overcoming faith that will rout out *church hurt* from your soul. This reading will inevitably produce in you a healthier, more spiritual, and pragmatic perspective of Christ and the Church that He will soon return to receive.

In the name of Jesus, I proclaim that you will be significantly enlightened, healed, delivered, and set free after having read this Holy Spirit–inspired book!

In Him,

Kenneth W. Davison Sr.
Founder & Senior Pastor,
New Life Church, San Antonio, Texas

INTRODUCTION

Christ's salvation is the most fascinating, monumental, and mind-altering journey imaginable. It is full of the most sacrificial exchanges and life changes one could ever experience. There is no other spiritual, mental, physical, exhilarating feeling or supernatural encounter that could even remotely compare to this type of massive takeover from our mighty God. Nothing in this world compares to this beautiful experience, and I highly recommend it!

The Christian Encounters
Lately, I have encountered so many hurting Christians from every type of church. Sadly, their stories are eerily similar when it comes to so many of the Church's (body of Christ's) indiscretions and growing issues. I have had countless conversations over the years with a growing number of people from different walks of life, denominations, and backgrounds (including pastors, Sunday school teachers, ministers, and lay members). Many of them have left a church organization, a ministry, a Christian fellowship, or the Christian faith altogether because they are tired of biblical compromising, hidden dishonesty, political culture, worldly entertainment, and preposterous programmed nonsense.

Unfortunately, these hurting people seem to have the same three main issues with the body of Christian believers.

The *primary* of these apparent concerns is, they fail to see *unconditional love* or the compassion of Christ from those who call upon the name of the Lord (they did not receive adequate personal assistance, heartfelt empathy, or direction during times of a spiritual dilemma).

Next, they want to know why there is no *direct accountability standard* for everyone in their church (especially when it comes to reprimanding certain people and rectifying the ungodly behaviors/attitudes of those holding positions).

Categorically, they do not see or feel the effects of the overwhelming power or leading of the Holy Spirit. He seemed to be absent from the weekly services. He was not active in those in the pulpit. Many in leadership positions had no spiritual discernment and were void of scriptural and life-changing messages. Others were following unbiblical doctrines and corrupt protocols. Others were too busy fleecing, beating, bleeding, and scattering the sheep to notice any additional problems.

Profoundly, the synopsis of 99 percent of these people's top Christian grievances were the lack of love, how people and church business were being handled (mishandled), and the absence of the Holy Spirit.

The Non-Christian Encounters
I have met and ministered to many people outside of the faith (including atheists and agnostics) who refuse to have anything to do with Christians, churches, or any organized religion due to what they may have seen or heard involving certain types of Christians or denominations.

Some unbelievers have rejected God or Christ because of what they have personally gone through in life, and they feel that God could have prevented their abuse. Numerous others reject God due to their home life involving *"Christian"* family members who *talked the talk* but failed to demonstrate the heart of Christ. Quite a few stayed away from the Christian faith due to satanically driven press reports and misinformed news media outlets, which often aim to paint Christians in a harmful light. The remainder stayed away or left because sin was far more enticing to them than applying and living the word of God. They find ways to blame God and condemn the Church and Christians to avoid changing or conducting self-evaluations.

We, as believers and Christ-followers, should not cause people to flee into the world. We should not chase them away from the sanctum of the Church, or let them remain in a sin-sick state as we practice continual un-Christlike behavior. We must show forth the heart of God and have the mind of Christ if we are going to succeed in Kingdom endeavors. **We must do our parts to snatch these souls from the fires of Hell. These are the most crucial times in history to win souls, make disciples for Christ, and not run lost souls closer toward Satan** (read Jude 1:17–23, Amplified Version).

"But as for you, beloved, remember the [prophetic] words spoken by the apostles of our Lord Jesus Christ. They used to say to you, 'In the last days there will be scoffers, following after their own ungodly passions.' These are the ones who are [agitators] causing divisions—worldly-minded [secular, unspiritual, carnal, merely sensual—unsaved], devoid of the Spirit. But you, beloved, build yourselves up on [the foundation of] your most holy faith [continually progress, rise like an edifice higher and higher], pray in the Holy Spirit, and keep yourselves in the love of God, waiting anxiously and looking forward to the mercy of our Lord Jesus Christ [which will bring you] to eternal life. And have mercy on some, who are doubting; save others, snatching them out of the fire; and on some have mercy but with fear, loathing even the clothing spotted and polluted by their shameless immoral freedom."

What Do the Scriptures Say?

You will inevitably see many scriptures repeated several times in this book and books to come, as they are worth repeating to gain more spiritual understanding.

I will clarify (through the scriptures) how we are to deal with one another and the unsaved. I will also show you where the Church has fallen short in its love, unity, and understanding of the truth. Matthew 7:12–23 is explained by Jesus as He teaches His disciples about some of the things I will cover further in this book (and the upcoming books to follow) regarding the difference between an authentic true Christian and a false (fake) Christian.

> *"So, whatever you wish that others would do to you, do also to them, for this is the Law and the Prophets. "Enter by the narrow gate. For the gate is wide and the way is easy that leads to destruction, and those who enter by it are many. For the gate is narrow and the way is hard that leads to life, and those who find it are few. "Beware of false prophets, who come to you in sheep's clothing but inwardly are ravenous wolves. You will recognize them by their fruits. Are grapes gathered from thorn bushes or figs from thistles? So, every healthy tree bears good fruit, but the diseased tree bears bad fruit. A healthy tree cannot bear bad fruit, nor can a diseased tree bear good fruit. Every tree that does not bear good fruit is cut down and thrown into the fire. Thus, you will recognize them by their fruits. Not everyone who says to me, 'Lord, Lord,' will enter the kingdom of heaven, but the one who does the will of my Father who is in heaven. On that day many will say to me, 'Lord, Lord, did we not prophesy in your name, and cast out demons in your name, and do many mighty works in your name?' And then will I declare to them, 'I never knew you; depart from me, you workers of lawlessness.'"*

Ephesians 5:1–2, says *"Be imitators of God...and live a life of love, just as Christ loved us and gave Himself up for us."* Suppose the lives of various churchgoers (leaders included) are not lining up with the word of God, or they are presenting false doctrine or exalting man's traditional religion above biblical truth. In that case, they are not to be trusted. Diligently watch, pray, and hear from the Spirit of God concerning how to deal with them because they need to be set free and delivered, so *beware*! You will know them by their fruit or lack thereof. If they do not continually show attributes of Christ, then Yahweh is not their Father! (See reference scriptures: John 15:1–27, Colossians 1:10, John chapter 8, and 1 John 3:8.)

Purpose

The main objective here is to help you see and understand what God's word says about the people who *seem* to be godly in form but have no Spirit-led power. These people make all Christians look bad and mess up others along the way. They are causing people to stumble and stray away from the faith, leave fellowships and the things of God.

"But understand this, that in the last days there will come times of difficulty.
For people will be lovers of self, lovers of money, proud, arrogant, abusive,
disobedient to their parents, ungrateful, unholy, heartless, unappeasable,
slanderous, without self-control, brutal, not loving good, treacherous, reckless,
swollen with conceit, lovers of pleasure rather than lovers of God, having the
appearance of godliness but denying its power.
Avoid such people."
(2 Tim. 3:15)

As you can see, 2 Timothy 3:1-5 prepares us for what is coming by telling us what to look out for during these crazy and unprecedented times. This scripture is not just referring to the sinner's behavior in this millennium. For centuries, these issues have been a reoccurring factor for "Christians" inside and outside every church's umbrella (I will further detail this passage of scripture in this book and those to follow).

Lamentably, many do not know what they are doing. Others know what they are doing and how they are hurting people but seem not to care. They are still lying to the people by misusing their gifts, displeasing God, and insulting Christ's work on the Cross by their words and actions.

Pretending Christians have no clue what it truly means to be an authentic representation of Christ (a genuine Christian disciple). They are spiritually deceived and devoid in their minds, diseased in their hearts, and besieged by Satan in their souls concerning the truth! Keep them in your prayers, and know that with or without them, our God will get the ultimate victory, Jesus will return and claim those who are His, and the Church will prevail!

I Write to You

This book will back up God's written word with the written word of God (2 Tim. 3:16). God cannot lie, and His holy word does not lie. He puts His holy word above His name (Heb. 6:13–20, Ps.138:2–4).

As you read further, you will undoubtedly begin to understand how to deal with or heal from any past, present, or future Church problems caused by others. You will continue to read and gain more knowledge and understanding about this subject of *Overcoming Church Hurt*. You will also discern what *you* may have done to cause unnecessary hurt to yourself and how to avoid or disallow any future harm to come upon you or those you love.

Maybe you are considering becoming a Christian and you are searching for answers, but you don't know where to turn or who to trust. Please do not put this book down! I desire you to get to know the only true and living God, not the one that the actions of Christian imposters have distorted. Christian or non-Christian, whether you attend a church or not, this book is for you!

Whether you tend to the ministry's parking lot or tend to *Christ's sheep*, this book is for you! This book is for you if you are a believer taking part in any Christian fellowship, services, outreaches, and any Christ-related programs, functions, or activities! Every church, every faith-based ministry, every denomination, and every congregation needs this book. I am writing to you because the Spirit of the living God wants to minister to you today.

I am writing to everyone who has ever been used, abused, misused, confused, or lied about by those who did not or do not truly represent Christ or the Church (His Bride) as the scriptures dictate. If a careless Christian has hurt you in any way, or you feel *All Churched Out*, then I wrote this book for you! **Yes, you!**

This book series is long overdue, yet it's right on time for such a time as this.

A Kingdom Mandate and Mission

The coming book series is almost two decades in the making. Therefore, I will *boldly*, uncompromisingly, and fearlessly follow the will of God concerning this matter. Just as Paul, James, and others had to speak the truth to and about the Church (as inspired by the Spirit), I too will write whatever the Holy Spirit leads and empowers me to write. I am in total allegiance and obedience to God's will and His word. I will not compromise because of people or their opinions. I did not ask for this undertaking; it was *purposed* to me.

This book is about allowing the Lord to open the eyes of the spiritually blinded. It is He who will break the chains of bondage that have held the Saints captive to foolishness. Writing to the Church of today is one of my Kingdom assignments. My God-given directive and holy missions are to reveal the truth and lead people into healing and divine restoration!

For the Record

I will not ever come against the word of God (prayerfully, the *word of God* will hit you where you need to be hit and heal you where you need to be healed)! I will not ever come against any individuals unrighteously, but I will not stop speaking the truth in love. I love God, Jesus, the Holy Spirit, and the *true* Bride/Body of Christ too much to ignore and not address the ongoing issues flagrantly allowed in Christendom.

Ephesians 6:12: ***"For we do not wrestle against flesh and blood, but against the rulers, against the authorities, against the cosmic powers over this present darkness, against the spiritual forces of evil in the heavenly places."*** If anyone gets mad about the truth, know this: I am not writing or speaking of my own volition or accord. This book is Holy Spirit–inspired! Jesus said to His disciples in John 16:13–14, ***"But when He, the Spirit of truth, comes, He will guide you into all the truth. He will not speak on his own; He will speak only what he hears, and He will tell you what is yet to come. He will glorify me because it is from me that He will receive what He will make known to you."*** Thus, the Holy Spirit will contend with every demonic spirit operating in those who hate spiritual truth in any form.

My spiritual intent is to reveal and expose all of the filth, lies, selfishness, misconceptions, greed, and the concealed sins that have been hindering the most powerful move of God in our churches for more than fifty years! These same familiar sins have caused redundant offenses and transgressions against God and Christ for far too long! The words of Christ have gone unapplied and unfulfilled for far too long!

All evil and sinister plots, schemes, and plans of the devil will no longer hinder the Body of Christ in the name of Jesus. Satan has no power against the anointed sons and daughters of the Most High God. I decree that Satan's reign over regions, territories, principalities, and churches will be exposed, expelled, and demilitarized by the Holy Spirit! Yahweh, my God, will be exalted, He will arise, and His enemies will be scattered, and the dynamic Church will arise and prevail in the name of Jesus, the Christ of Nazareth!

So fasten your seat belts, as you will read many truthful and (un)known things that will finally be unmasked and revealed. You will better understand the types of people who call themselves Christians or Children of God, yet their hearts, words, and actions are far from Christ. You will see what has been covered up extensively by charisma, ornate clothing, collars, conferences, convocations, powerless sermons and prayer lines, fancy footwork, loud music, and prophetic gifts for too many years.

May God (Yahweh) greatly bless you and keep you protected in every way. May He make His glorious face shine upon you and be mercifully gracious toward you in abundance as He looks upon you with pleasurable favor and gives you His incomprehensible peace (Num. 6:24–26). So be it, and it is so in Jesus's name. Amen.

See you on victory lane!
[There are at least fifty different scriptures used in this book for you to reference, study, and apply. Please use them in your everyday living.]

Church Saved or Soul Saved?

I received Christ and got saved (born again, for real) around the age of twenty-five. I say "for real" because that is when I ultimately gave my heart, body, spirit, and soul to God without reservations. That is also when I had a real encounter with God and my life began to change for the better (John 3:1–8,16; Rom. chapters 6, 8, and 10). Before then, I did not know God for myself. I did not understand biblical salvation, but I knew church salvation all too well.

What Being Saved Is Not

My mother was a true example of a holy woman of God, a devoted Christian, and a missionary for God. She was a sincere model of a loving and respectful wife and mother. She kept me in the church from birth until adulthood, and she taught me by example, not mere words. She taught me how to pray and how to live for God at an early age. She did not play with God! My mother did not play with the Bible; she did not play church, nor did she play with people who played church! My mother would often say, "Either you are in or you are out. Pick a side; you cannot be on the fence. Do not play with God" (the devil owns the fence and the middle ground).

I knew what it looked like to be *saved*, sanctified, and filled with the precious Holy Ghost. I knew what being *sold out* to Jesus meant and how holy living behind closed doors was supposed to look. I knew there was a difference between going to church and being a disciple of Christ. I grew up knowing not to straddle the fence or *play saved* (but I did attempt the *born-again* thing a few times to see if I was ready to commit, and I was not).

Yes, I confessed with my mouth, and I *somewhat* believed in my heart that Christ was the risen Savior and the Son of God (Rom. 10:9–10). I was not saved by biblical standards (a disciple of Christ)! I "accepted" Him for who the church said He was, but I did not *receive* Him or clearly understand what He had come to do in me and my life. My entire heart did not belong to God (as I was trying to serve two masters and still go to heaven). Parts of my life and soul only belonged to God on *most* Sundays, but the other parts belonged to the world on the six other days. I knew worldly standards could not save me. Comfortable church atmospheres will permit an unholy spirit to do anything, thus making worldview-salvation seem acceptable (the norm for many Sabbath-keeping and Sunday worshippers of today).

As a young adult, I, too, was in that misguided group of unsaved "Christians" who confessed to Christ but did not possess a holy relationship with Christ. I believed in Him, but I was too worldly to completely follow Him because my out-of-church lifestyle seemed more rewarding and fun (as many of my Sabbath-observing and Sunday-morning peers thought). I wanted to live in both worlds—the regular world and the church world. I felt I was *too young* to give up the clubs, the streets, and the sin I was addicted to practicing.

I grew up watching other people "do church" (fake salvation), and act as if their "church clothes" or going to church Tuesday through Sunday would cover their wicked deeds and fleshly lusts. So, I effortlessly conformed to being what I call "church saved". The church saved groups consist of the young and the old who think being active in church equates to biblical salvation. They are a step above "church-goers" (those who come to be seen and stir up the most mess), yet a step below biblical (true) salvation. They do enough to make people *think* they genuinely love the Lord. Most church leaders fail to address or correct this world-view-salvation out of fear of losing members or becoming unpopular. The Saints rarely dare to challenge or confront this most deceitful group of pretenders, as the *church-saved* population works amongst the best of them.

As a young girl, I *accepted* Christ as my friend, but I did not spend much time getting to know Him. As a teenager, I *accepted* Christ again as a ticket out of Hell, but I did not change my ways or trust Him with my life. At twenty-two, I went through some challenges, so I went to the altar during church to "get saved" again (because the last two times were like bad perms...they did not take)! If things went well with my life, I stuck to *salvation*. When things fell apart, I was back to my old worldly lifestyle of sinful fun (yes, sin was fun, enticing, and pleasurable for a season, but there is a hefty price, Rom. 6:23). Honestly, I was not ready to walk away from the world.

Again, I had "accepted" Christ as the Savior for humankind, but I did not *receive* Him as *my* Lord, nor did I invest any time in my profession of salvation or pursue a relationship with Him. I did not have a made-up mind when it came to living as a Christian. Therefore, I do not count those moments of mediocre and insincere public confessions of salvation before age twenty-five. A true rebirth requires genuine repentance, a new (clean) heart, a renewed mind, and an overpowering desire to turn from sin permanently; I had none of those things. I was not saved at all!

Still Not Saved!

As a young adult fresh out of high school, I dressed up and went to church religiously every Sunday (and I still was not saved). I paid tithes, gave offerings, clapped, jumped, raised my hands, praised the Lord, and said "amen" on cue (and I still was not saved). I learned how to cry out to God for help through prayer when my life got too rough. I would repent long enough for a breakthrough (blessed but still not saved). I went to church events around the city, and all my close friends knew I loved going to church (still not saved). I knew every gospel song word for word, I could pray like the elders, and I could get emotionally charged with the best of them (and I still was not saved, sanctified, set free, or delivered).

If anyone asked me, I would tell them without a doubt, "I am a Christian, and I love God!"

> *"Do not love the world or the things in the world. If anyone loves the world, the love of the Father is not in him. For all that is in the world—the desires of the flesh and the desires of the eyes and pride of life—is not from the Father but is from the world. And the world is passing away along with its desires, but whoever does the will of God abides forever."*
> (1 John 2:15–17)

Like so many others, I was *intelligently ignorant* concerning salvation because I was faithful but not committed! Like so many others, I was living a lie, and I was not serious about pleasing God, maturing in Christ, or growing in the word. **Like so many others, I only succeeded in church culture but not in Christ.** Like so many others, I only wanted Christ to be my human resources manager, but not the CEO of my life. Like so many others, I was on my way to Hell (long skirt and all) because I not only desired to continue living *my way*, but I also enjoyed going to clubs, parties, and hanging out late at night while dating God on Sundays. Like so many others, my lukewarm, young adult Christian lifestyle was good enough for me because I was not as bad as others I knew (deceived again).

Reflexively I could do all the right *churchy* things, but my heart was in going to a church, not going to the word of God. My church lifestyle had not changed much since birth, so of course, I learned to conform to the culture. I was not transformed; I was conditioned to the behaviors, but I was not saved (just as many of you reading this today)! My love was belonging to an organization and not belonging to the Kingdom of righteousness. I had a religious and adulterous relationship with Sunday services and church activities, but not a committed and intimate relationship with Christ Jesus as Lord of my life. I loved *churchy* people, places, and things, but applying that love solely to the things of God was nonexistent. I would live how I wanted to live Monday through Saturday night (sometimes even early Sunday morning), then come to church for my weekly affair on the pew and my emotional *fix in the mix*. I was addicted to a form of godliness, but there was no power in my life. I was not doing the will of the Father (truthfully, at least 60 percent of the "faithful" Saints have no Holy Ghost power either, because many of them are living a lie today just like I was back then).

I knew I was only a Christian by association, not a Christian by Christlike standards. I knew I was just church saved and nothing more because I was still *practicing sin on purpose*! I knew not to lead in ministry works or minister to people like I was sanctified or living the "Christ-life" myself. I knew it was hypocritical to talk and not live the part; I knew I was not saved (1 John 2:4–10).

After a few years of worldly observation, this kind-hearted "church girl" had become enamored with the ways of the streets. I had a gift to learn and discern people early on in my life, and the devil wanted to use me to carry out his devious plans, then destroy me as a young adult! I was inclined to live my way and do what I thought made me happy, not holy. I was slowly self-destructing in the "fast life."

At twenty-four, after going through life's trials and disappointments, Satan convinced me to go deeper into sin by indulging more in a lifestyle of the streets. The plans he had for me sounded like excellent and prosperous plans to live a better life. I prepared myself, and the following Monday would be the day I stepped up to bat as Satan's lead hitter!

I was planning to keep going to church, praising, and thanking God like a decent *churchgoing* individual (that is the mentality of a church-saved but not soul-saved people). I loved the Lord, but the world was calling me louder than He was at the time. Honestly, I wanted to see if the world had a better offer on the table (I was still trying to serve two masters, still not saved).

I went to church that Sunday (as usual), but this Sunday would be different because I had a specific purpose for going. I was only going to repent for what I was planning to do on Monday. I wanted *premeditated forgiveness* for the deliberate sin I intended to commit the following Monday. I was hoping God would have mercy on me and allow things to work in my favor without me getting hurt or killed in the process. I believed He would protect me because I was still a good person, even though my secret life was ungodly (more lies, more deception).

Premeditated Sin

Let me take a moment to address *pre-repentance*
(repenting for deliberate sin). I want to give you some clear definitions
and an understanding of what *premeditation* and *sin* mean. Then I want
to help you see them in the Light the word of God brings.

Sin: Any act regarded as a transgression against God. A willful or
unwillful violation of God's will. A deliberate or unintentional violation of a religious principle. An immoral standard which opposes the
holy scriptures and God's holy nature, province, and sovereignty.

The Bible defines *sin* as lawlessness or the breaking or transgression of
God's divine law and commandments. It is also described as disobedience or rebellion against God, His Holy Word, and His will. Sin is of
the devil, and death is the disconsolate reward (Rom. 6:23). Sin is doing
what is wrong or not doing what is right according to the mandates of
God's Holy Word (these are called sins of omission and sins of commission, whether out of defiant disregard or ignorance).

*"Everyone who makes a practice of sinning also practices
lawlessness; sin is lawlessness. You know that he appeared*

to take away sins, and in him there is no sin. No one who abides in him keeps on sinning; no one who keeps on sinning has either seen him or known him. Little children let no one deceive you. Whoever practices righteousness is righteous, as he is righteous. Whoever makes a practice of sinning is of the devil, for the devil has been sinning from the beginning. The reason the Son of God appeared was to destroy the works of the devil. No one born of God makes a practice of sinning, for God's seed abides in him; and he cannot keep on sinning because he has been born of God. By this it is evident who are the children of God, and who are the children of the devil: whoever does not practice righteousness is not of God, nor is the one who does not love his brother." (1 John 2:4–10)

If God's word says, "Do not lie, do not steal, do not kill, do not fornicate, do not commit adultery," and you do those things (knowingly or unknowingly), you have sinned against God and His word, thus making you a sinner.

Sin is a satanically driven influence. Sin separates you from God, who is Light (but sin does not separate you from God's unconditional and everlasting love (Rom. 8:31–39)). Sin separates you from God because it opposes His perfect will or designed order of holy living; if this were not true, there would be no need for Christ or reconciliation to God.

"For if while we were enemies we were reconciled to God through the death of His Son, it is much more [certain], now that we are reconciled, that we shall be saved (daily delivered from sin's dominion) through His [resurrection] life. Not only so, but we also rejoice and exultingly glory in God [in His love and perfection] through our Lord Jesus Christ, through Whom we have now received and enjoy [our] reconciliation."
(Rom. 5:10–11 Amplified)

"But all things are from God, Who through Jesus Christ reconciled us to Himself [received us into favor, brought us into harmony with Himself] and gave to us the ministry of reconciliation [that by word and deed we might aim to bring others into harmony with Him]. It was God [personally present] in Christ, reconciling and restoring the world to favor with Himself, not counting up and holding against [men] their trespasses [but cancelling them], and committing to us the message of reconciliation (of the restoration to favor). So we are Christ's ambassadors, God making His appeal as it were through us. We [as Christ's personal representatives] beg you for His sake to lay hold of the divine favor [now offered you] and be reconciled to God." (2 Cor. 5:18–21, Amplified)

"And although you were at one time estranged and alienated and hostile-minded [toward Him], participating in evil things, yet Christ has now reconciled you [to God] in His physical body through death, in order to present you before the Father holy and blameless and beyond reproach [and He will do this] if you continue in the faith, well-grounded and steadfast, and not shifting away from the [confident] hope [that is a result] of the gospel that you have heard, which was proclaimed in all creation under heaven, and of which [gospel] I, Paul, was made a minister." (Col. 1:21–23, Amplified)

Sin is darkness, and sin hates the light, which is God's truth, God's way. Anything corrupt and wicked cannot abide in the light of God's glorious presence, *"And the Light shines on in the darkness, for the darkness has never overpowered it [put it out or absorbed it or appropriated it and is unreceptive to it]"* (John 1:5, Amplified). Light and darkness cannot coexist. They are two different events with two different purposes and agendas. Light overpowers darkness, but darkness must be introduced to the Light. God's word, power, and glory shining through Jesus is that light!

> *"This is the message we have heard from him and proclaim to you, that God is light, and in him is no darkness at all."* (1 John 1:5)

> *"Again, Jesus spoke to them, saying, 'I am the light of the world. Whoever follows me will not walk in darkness, but will have the light of life.'"* (John 8:12)

> *"But if we walk in the light, as he is in the light, we have fellowship with one another, and the blood of Jesus his Son cleanses us from all sin."* (1 John 1:7)

> *"But you are a chosen race, a royal priesthood, a holy nation, a people for his own possession, that you may proclaim the excellencies of him who called you out of darkness into his marvelous light."* (1 Pet. 2:9)

Repentance: A decisive and willful change in direction. A shift or turning from one path or course to another. Compunction or deep regret leads to a change of heart, mind, and life. When the power of the Holy Spirit convicts and confronts a person's soul (mind, will, and emotions), leading to a holy conversion. A humbling, shameful, guilt-ridden sorrow for an act of sin, leading to a critical transformation of one's life through salvation.

Having great remorse and regret for intentional or unintentional transgressions against God, people, or self. Repentance produces a godly conviction, a changed heart and righteousness (not condemnation). You will want to turn away from sin and seek the Lord for forgiveness, healing, and redemption when you have sincerely repented.

According to Psalm 51:17, David defines *repentance* as something that stems from having a genuinely broken spirit and repentant heart toward God concerning the sin(s) committed. He wrote this after committing adultery and murder: *"My [only] sacrifice [acceptable] to God is a broken spirit; A broken and contrite heart [broken with sorrow for sin, thoroughly penitent], such, O God, You will not despise"* (Amplified version).

A contrite heart is when a person is broken to the point that causes them to wholeheartedly change direction and pursue the things of God (openly and privately). A revelation of God's truth and God's love will lead to a broken heart and a contrite spirit or penitence (repentance). Too many people are confused and deceived, and they do not understand true repentance.

There are two conditions of repentance; you must turn toward God (righteousness) and turn away from sin (unrighteousness). Please take time to read 2 Chronicles 7:14; Matthew 3:8 and 4:17; Luke 5:32 and 13:3; Acts 3:19, 11:18, and 17:29–31; 2 Peter 3:9; 1 John 1:9; and Revelation 2:5. After reading those scriptures, you should have a better understanding of repentance.

Premeditation: The action of plotting or planning something (especially a crime).

Specific intent or consideration that shows intent to commit a lawful or an unlawful act. The anticipation to follow through with a plot or plan.

Synonyms: criminal intent · malice · forethought· preplanning · prearrangement · deliberation · scheming

Premeditation of sin and pre-repentance is evil at work in your heart and mind!

Premeditation of sin acknowledges that you purposely plan to sin against God in some form or fashion despite spiritual forfeits. Understand that this type of reasoning is fraudulent and misled thinking influenced by spiritual wickedness at work in you. This mentality directly acknowledges that *you know that what you are about to do is sinful and wrong.* Yet, you are determined to follow through with Satan's plans for your life regardless of the possible ramifications without recourse (many times without genuine remorse or change following the action).

Pre-repentance is when you have already made up your mind to do unjustly, but you want the Lord to forgive you before committing the violation or act of wickedness. For example, pre-repentance is asking God to look away and excuse or pardon you before (or while) you have sex outside of His ordained marital boundaries. Another example is when you have decisively planned to rob, steal, kill, lie, cheat, or deceive. Still, you have a conscience to pray for forgiveness or mercy preceding your crime against God but not a conscience to desist or a desire to resist. **Pre-repentance is a deliberate crime against God and an act of disobedience and rebellion!** However, you can certainly pray and repent for allowing the temptation to become your heart's desire to sin. Just know God does not honor pre-repentance from a heart willing to defy and disobey His holy will.

The mindset of pre-repentance will undoubtedly lead to spiritual, physical, mental, and many times deadly penalties with eternal consequences if not renewed, corrected, and abandoned!

> *"You adulterous people! Do you not know that friendship with the world is enmity with God? Therefore, whoever wishes to be a friend of the world makes himself an enemy of God. Or do you suppose it is to no purpose that the scripture says, "He yearns jealously over the spirit that he has made to dwell in us"? But he gives more grace. Therefore, it says, "God opposes*

the proud but gives grace to the humble." Submit yourselves therefore to God. Resist the devil, and he will flee from you. Draw near to God, and he will draw near to you. Cleanse your hands, you sinners, and purify your hearts, you double-minded." (James 4:4–8)

"... whoever desires to love life and see good days, let him keep his tongue from evil and his lips from speaking deceit; let him turn away from evil and do good; let him seek peace and pursue it. For the eyes of the Lord are on the righteous, and his ears are open to their prayer. But the face of the Lord is against those who do evil." (1 Peter 3:10–12)

The Old and New Testaments state that God will not respond to those indulging in evil and refuse to repent, and He repeatedly asks us to turn from evil and follow righteousness. (Read 2 Chronicles 7:14, Proverbs 1:24–28 and 28:9, Isaiah 59:1–2, Daniel 9:13–14, Micah 3:4, 1 Peter 3:12, 1 Timothy 6:10–11, 2 Timothy 2:22, and 1 John 1:9.)

Premeditated sin is a dangerous and lethal road that will ultimately lead to damnation if no detour is taken. You do not want to retain a conscience that loves to practice sin or desires to go against God at any cost. The penalty is a reprobate mind, death, then Hell! Romans 1:28 uses the phrase "reprobate mind" when referring to those whom God has allowed to remain corrupt as they continue to resist Him. They will not acknowledge the truth of Christ's work on the Cross. Therefore, they have decided to remain sinful, godless, and wicked despite the terrible and deadly costs. Sadly, these people are blinded to the truth at the hands of Satan.

"To the pure, all things are pure, but to the defiled and unbelieving, nothing is pure; but both their minds and their consciences are defiled. They profess to know God, but they

deny him by their works. They are detestable, disobedient, unfit for any good work." (Titus 1:15–16)

These scriptures are referring to the types of people who profess to love and know God (church saved). Yet they have selfish hearts and desires that they continue to carry out; therefore, they are just like unbelievers. They are perishing as well. They think their excuses, self-seeking motives, and ungodly agendas justify their moral corruption. Their lies, hatred, double-minded practices, sexual sins, and all other forms of immorality go against the characteristics of a true believer (disciple).

God's Wrath on Unrighteousness

"For the wrath of God is revealed from heaven against all ungodliness and unrighteousness of men, who by their unrighteousness suppress the truth. For what can be known about God is plain to them, because God has shown it to them. For his invisible attributes, namely, his eternal power and divine nature, have been clearly perceived, ever since the creation of the world, in the things that have been made. So they are without excuse. For although they knew God, they did not honor him as God or give thanks to him, but they became futile in their thinking, and their foolish hearts were darkened. Claiming to be wise, they became fools, and exchanged the glory of the immortal God for images resembling mortal man and birds and animals and creeping things. Therefore God gave them up in the lusts of their hearts to impurity, to the dishonoring of their bodies among themselves, because they exchanged the truth about God for a lie and worshiped and served the creature rather than the Creator, who is blessed forever! Amen." (Rom. 1:18-25, KJV)

"For this reason God gave them up to dishonorable passions. For their women exchanged natural relations for those that are contrary to nature; and the men likewise gave up natural relations with women and were consumed with passion for one another, men committing shameless acts with men and receiving in themselves the due penalty for their error. And since they did not see fit to acknowledge God, God gave them up to a debased mind to do what ought not to be done. They were filled with all manner of unrighteousness, evil, covetousness, malice. They are full of envy, murder, strife, deceit, maliciousness. They are gossips, slanderers, haters of God, insolent, haughty, boastful, inventors of evil, disobedient to parents, foolish, faithless, heartless, ruthless. Though they know God's righteous decree that those who practice such things deserve to die, they not only do them but give approval to those who practice them." (Rom. 1:18–32, ESV)

"Therefore, having this ministry by the mercy of God, we do not lose heart. But we have renounced disgraceful, underhanded ways. We refuse to practice cunning or to tamper with God's word, but by the open statement of the truth we would commend ourselves to everyone's conscience in the sight of God. And even if our gospel is veiled, it is veiled to those who are perishing. In their case, the god of this world has blinded the minds of the unbelievers, to keep them from seeing the light of the gospel of the glory of Christ, who is the image of God." (2 Cor. 4:1–4, ESV)

WARNING: Please do not be deceived! Do not allow your heart to wax cold, become indifferent or callous to the word of God due to your negligence or the misbehaviors of others. You have a way of escape! You do not have to remain stuck where you are spiritually; it is futile not to sincerely repent with your whole heart today, as you will be held accountable for what you know. You have been warned, given scriptures and examples of what the living God requires of you. I urge you to heed every scripture in this chapter and meditate on them, as you will see many of these scriptures again throughout this book.

> *"Blessed is the man who remains steadfast under trial, for when he has stood the test, he will receive the crown of life, which God has promised to those who love him. Let no one say when he is tempted, 'I am being tempted by God,' for God cannot be tempted with evil, and he himself tempts no one. But each person is tempted when he is lured and enticed by his desire. Then desire when it has conceived gives birth to sin, and sin, when it is fully grown brings forth death. Do not be deceived, my beloved brothers."* (James 1:12–16)

> *"Therefore submit to God. Resist the devil, and he will flee from you. Draw near to God and He will draw near to you. Cleanse your hands, you sinners, and purify your hearts, you double-minded. Lament and mourn and weep! Let your laughter be turned to mourning and your joy to gloom. Humble yourselves in the sight of the Lord, and He will lift you up."* (James 4:7–10, NKJV)

The Wonder of Salvation

The following Sunday morning, after my weekend of premeditations, I woke up and got dressed for church. A new Elder came from New York that morning, and he preach like the Apostle Paul. He had such an enthusiastic and compelling testimony of how he allowed Christ to enter his life. There was a burning fire in his eyes (they turned red while he preached) and an inexplicable fire in his preaching. I had never seen or heard anyone with such strength and conviction in my entire church life! There was something different about him; he made me want to hear more about this Jesus he so passionately spoke. The more this man preached, the more I *almost* wanted to get saved for real! I was captivated by the evident presence of the power of God in his life. That same power was taking over the atmosphere around me!

I was so engulfed by what I heard and felt this preacher saying that I could not even grasp all of his words. I was in a trance of some sort because I could see the Holy Spirit moving around him. I could feel the Holy Spirit's presence, to the point where I started to repent for what I was planning to do on Monday. Then something happened!

I was sitting at the end of my row near the back with my head down, talking to God. I looked up, and this fiery preaching machine was walking toward my area. I quickly put my head down again, hoping it was not me he was coming for, but it was! I looked up again, and there he stood in front of me with eyes of fire, telling me that God wanted all of me! To my surprise, he began to openly reveal my plans for Monday and how the enemy would use me and trap me. I was shocked that this stranger knew my *premeditated* plans, because I had not told anyone about my intentions! This man heard from God, prayed in tongues, and interpreted what he prayed. I was perplexed about how God could use anyone in this manner. I knew it was real because he did not know me! God sent him to me out of all the other people in the church!

This preacher kept talking to me and speaking well of Christ, then immediately I heard the devil say, "You are not ready to get saved today; ignore him." But I could not ignore him! I could not look away from the Light around Him or deny the Holy Spirit within this man of God. There was such a powerful force and an undeniable strength coming from this man until I started to shake and cry in my seat. Then he stretched out his hand toward me and said, "Today is the day of salvation." I looked up at his hand, and he said, "What will it be, life or death?" I sat there staring into space until he said, "Choose life in Christ today and live for God, for tomorrow is not promised," and at that moment, I stood up for God, and I chose life!

I took his hand as we walked to the front of the church together. I cried from deep within my soul. I had a broken spirit and a contrite heart toward the Lord for the first time. I remember feeling absolute joy, complete peace, and the incomprehensible love of God like I had never felt before! I finally had an exhilarating encounter with the God of my salvation, I surrendered all, and my life changed forever!

Saved, Saved, Saved!

I had finally received Christ as my Savior, Lord, and Master of my soul! **I was saved for real this time; I not only felt it, but I also knew it!** I was overcome with endless emotions of awe, as I finally had a new heart, a heart that desired God over sin! I had willingly made up my mind to trust Him and His holy word. I not only confessed my sins but also repented (turned away from practicing sin) and renounced them once and for all (1 John 1:9, Acts 3:17–26). I decisively made a 180-degree turn from my carnal and worldly ways because I wanted to walk with God as Enoch and Noah once did (Gen. 5:21–24, 6:9; Col. 2:6–7). I desired to fully please and glorify God as my Father and Christ Jesus as my Redeemer, Lord, and King (James 1:21-25)!

Things about Jesus began to become alive in me as I tried to understand why Jesus would choose to save someone like me from the brink of total darkness and a path of sinful existence. How could God love and care so much for me that He would exchange His Son's life for mine? My mind could not conceive why He chose to be beaten and die for me before I was born? Why did the Son of God take the keys to death and Hell and overcome the grave for me? How could the power of God's unconditional love for me raise Christ from the dead? Why didn't He just let me die in my sins? The short answer to every question was and is *love*!

> *"For we ourselves were once foolish, disobedient, led astray, slaves to various passions and pleasures, passing our days in malice and envy, hated by others and hating one another. But when the goodness and loving kindness of God our Savior appeared, he saved us, not because of works done by us in righteousness, but according to his own mercy, by the washing of regeneration and renewal of the Holy Spirit, whom he poured out on us richly through Jesus Christ our Savior, so that being justified by his grace, we might become heirs according to the hope of eternal life."* (Titus 3:4–7, ESV)

Reading passages of scripture like this would make me think of Jesus and all He has done for me. Thoughts of His loving-kindness, grace, and mercy toward me would cause overflowing joy to fill my soul! I would cry like a newborn baby because of the sacrifice He made for me (and I still cry). I was so relieved and grateful to finally have Jesus in my life for real, for good, and forever! I was truly saved by grace through faith!

"For while we were still weak, at the right time Christ died for the ungodly." (Rom. 5:6, ESV)

For by grace you have been saved through faith. And this is not your own doing; it is the gift of God, not a result of works, so that no one may boast. (Eph. 2:8–9, ESV)

My sins were imputed to Him, and His righteousness was assigned to me. I was now a justifiable witness of my Savior's work on the Cross and His resurrection (2 Cor. 5:21; Rom. 3:20, 4:25). My faith validated my experience with Christ, and Christ justified my experience by faith.

"Therefore, since we have been justified by faith, we have peace with God through our Lord Jesus Christ. Through him we have also obtained access by faith into this grace in which we stand, and we rejoiced in hope of the glory of God." (Rom. 5:1, ESV)

Changed

Right away, I desired to live for God and follow Christ unreservedly. I searched for Jesus in the scriptures to learn how to hear His still voice in my spirit. I didn't know as much about Christ as I thought, so I wanted to gain more wisdom and knowledge about His will and my purpose. I wanted to daily converse with Him like He was my best friend, guidance counselor, or a parent who would help and teach me how to order my life. I now understood what it meant to be born again (John 3:1–8, 1 Pet. 1:22–25).

I had an instant love for Him that I had never had before, and this love was different. It made me want to get closer to Him each passing day. His relentless passion, generous grace, and multiplying mercy had been protecting me for years, and now I wanted to pursue Him! This kind of affection was new to me, but Galatians 2:20 clearly explains this encounter, this new birth and new nature experience (which transformed the old me into the better me).

> *"I have been crucified with Christ [in Him I have shared His crucifixion]. It is no longer I who live, but Christ (the Messiah) lives in me; and the life I now live in the body I live by faith in (by adherence to and reliance on and complete trust in) the Son of God, Who loved me and gave Himself up for me."* (Gal. 2:20, Amplified)

> *"If then you have been raised with Christ, seek the things that are above, where Christ is, seated at the right hand of God. Set your minds on things that are above, not on things that are on earth. For you have died, and your life is hidden with Christ in God. When Christ who is your life appears, then you also will appear with him in glory."* (Col. 3:1–4, ESV)

For the first time, the old Vanessa was dying daily to herself and her worldly desires (Luke 9:23, Gal. 5:24). The new Vanessa was rescued from the dominion of darkness. I had been received into the Kingdom of the Son of God (Col. 1:9–14). All the money in the world could not buy this type of "new birth" experience! I had a supernatural encounter with the living God, and it was a tremendous eye-opener and permanent game-changer! I felt content and not discouraged, whole and no longer broken.

There was a sense of deep inner peace within my mind, and no longer was a war raging. I joyfully praised my Savior for His sweet comfort and beautiful serenity! I was in a real relationship with my soul's Benefactor.

"For those who live according to the flesh set their minds on the things of the flesh, but those who live according to the Spirit set their minds on the things of the Spirit. For to set the mind on the flesh is death, but to set the mind on the Spirit is life and peace. For the mind that is set on the flesh is hostile to God, for it does not submit to God's law; indeed, it cannot. Those who are in the flesh cannot please God." (Rom. 8:5–8)

"Blessed be the God and Father of our Lord Jesus Christ! According to his great mercy, he has caused us to be born again to a living hope through the resurrection of Jesus Christ from the dead, to an inheritance that is imperishable, undefiled, and unfading, kept in heaven for you, who by God's power are being guarded through faith for a salvation ready to be revealed in the last time. In this you rejoice, though now for a little while, if necessary, you have been grieved by various trials, so that the tested genuineness of your faith—more precious than gold that perishes though it is tested by fire—may be found to result in praise and glory and honor at the revelation of Jesus Christ. Though you have not seen him, you love him. Though you do not now see him, you believe in him and rejoice with joy that is inexpressible and filled with glory, obtaining the outcome of your faith, the salvation of your souls." (1 Pet. 1:3–9)

I wanted to change everything! I first had to rectify my wrong-thinking and actions in the sight of God (the clean-up, mind renewal, or sanctification process). I refused to let the cowardly justification phrase "No one is perfect" become my excuse to continue practicing what I knew in my heart was wrong (sinful and ungodly behavior). I was determined not to allow the carnal statement "I am only human" to deter or limit me from living and doing my best for God after receiving His best (His Son, Yeshua).

> *"Strip yourselves of your former nature [put off and discard your old unrenewed self] which characterized your previous manner of life and becomes corrupt through lusts and desires that spring from delusion, and be constantly renewed in the spirit of your mind [having a fresh mental and spiritual attitude], and put on the new nature (the regenerate self) created in God's image, [Godlike] in true righteousness and holiness."* (Eph. 4:22–24, Amplified)

I allowed the Creator of all that is good to be my Heavenly Father. The only true and living God, El Shaddai, the All-Sufficient One, the Almighty God, who reigns supreme was now my God, guide, and complete source of security and life dependency. I was ready to receive all that is good and perfect for my life (James 1:17–18)! I was now reconciled and engrafted into the family of God (Rom. 11:11–31)! I was developing wonderfully, and soon there was an emergence of a spiritual "butterfly." Read how Paul explains the unveiling, morphing, converting, and this life-changing commission to the church of Corinth in the passages that follow.

> *"So, from now on, we regard no one from a human point of view [according to worldly standards and values]. Though we have known Christ from a human point of view, now we no longer know Him in this way. Therefore, if anyone is in Christ [that is, grafted in, joined to Him by faith in Him as Savior], he is a new creature [reborn and renewed by the Holy Spirit]; the old things [the previous moral and spiritual condition] have passed away. Behold, new things have come*

[because spiritual awakening brings a new life]. But all these things are from God, who reconciled us to Himself through Christ[making us acceptable to Him] and gave us the ministry of reconciliation[so that by our example we might bring others to Him], that is, that God was in Christ reconciling the world to Himself, not counting people's sins against them[but canceling them]. And He has committed to us the message of reconciliation[that is, restoration to favor with God]." (Cor. 5:16–19, Amplified)

I desired God's Spirit and power to work mightily in me. I wanted Him to operate powerfully through me more than I wanted to breathe. I wanted Him more than all the riches in the world, more than a husband, children, or the old life that I once enjoyed. My heart was fixed, my mind was renewed, and I was undeniably a converted, born-again Christ-follower!

Spirit-Filled

I became a woman in full pursuit of the colossal heart of God Almighty, as I was 100 percent convinced and willing to trust Him with all of my heart (Prov. 3:5–8). I wanted to live every waking moment in the center of His perfect will for my life. My heart and soul began to yearn for more fire and spiritual passion, more love, intimacy, communication, teaching, and excitement (I did not want to be a powerless pew-warming Christian).

God radically transformed me and was enthusiastically changing me daily. He was spiritually grooming and pruning me for His glory. I got baptized (immersed in water) a short time afterward (Mark 16:15–20), and I was filled with the Holy Spirit and fire before long.

"I baptize you with water for repentance, but he who is coming after me is mightier than I, whose sandals I am not worthy

to carry. He will baptize you with the Holy Spirit and fire."
(Matt. 3:11)

The *infilling* of the Holy Spirit amplified my Christian walk immensely!
There was indisputable evidence and signs following this wondrous
work! I despised my shameful and the adversative God-conscience I
once had, as the Holy Spirit helped me to see why sin had me sturdily
bound for so many years. I sought to allow the Spirit of God to free me
from all resistant and returning soul bondage and questionable deeds
that plagued me, as I did not want to grieve God or the Holy Spirit. I
needed to be delivered entirely from my old self by faith, and I needed to
be sanctified and deliberately seek to keep the "strongman" of demonic
oppression out of my life. (Eph. 4:30–31).

The Tangible Connection

This new-birth experience (salvation) combined with the fire of the Holy
Spirit (the source of godly transformation and power) is still one of the
most amazing times of my entire life to date. I felt like Clark Kent walking
around knowing that Superman was on the inside of me, but this was no
fairy tale or fictional experience. There was not only a tangible connec-
tion to God through faith in Christ, but there was also an intangible and
activated force working on the inside, waiting to be expressed outwardly.

I asked God for a more substantial encounter from the Holy Spirit, and
it began to happen. I asked Him to teach me, help me, lead me, train
me, and use me unlimitedly, and it began to happen! It all started to
happen as I began to use my faith to apply the following life-changing
scriptures: Mat. 6:33, 7:7-9, and Mk. 11:23-24.

> *"But seek first the kingdom of God and his righteousness, and
> all these things will be added to you."*

"Ask, and it will be given to you; seek, and you will find; knock, and it will be opened to you. For everyone who asks receives, the one who seeks finds, and to the one who knocks it will be opened."

"And Jesus answered them, 'Have faith in God. Truly, I say to you, whoever says to this mountain, "Be taken up and thrown into the sea," and does not doubt in his heart, but believes that what he says will come to pass, it will be done for him. Therefore, I tell you, whatever you ask in prayer, believe that you have received] it, and it will be yours.'"

I had been a living witness to the divine transformation in the lives of others, but now others would be a witness of His glory and power in my life! I had undeniable proof (not just words) that God was indeed real. The Christ-life was the best life, and the Holy Spirit was alive and active in me! From little faith to great faith, I soon went from a *little-light* Christian to a *bright-light* Christ-following disciple! For the first time in my life, I felt so undeservedly blessed, fulfilled, and overwhelmed at the same time! This phenomenal sensation was indescribable, inexplicable, and it continually increased in me daily (as I willingly surrendered and yielded myself and my selfish ways to Him).

[Woefully, many do not believe the Holy Spirit awaits to operate in *every* Christ-follower in a similar or greater manner. They have not thoroughly or unreservedly studied the scriptures for illumination. They have not intently prayed for divine revelation; study Mk. chapters 15, 16, 20; Acts chapters 1-3; and 1 Cor. chapters 12-14.]

The presence of the Holy Spirit was so alive and tangible to the point I felt strong and not weak; I felt hopeful and not helpless for the first time in my life. He made me appreciate the life and sacrifice of Christ even more. He helped me to read and understand the scriptures better.

He showed me how Jesus was not only my Savior but also my Lord, Brother, and Friend!

But Wait, There's More!

After being filled with the wonderful Holy Spirit, I prayed for every spiritual gift God wanted me to have and for Him to cultivate and help me to produce all the *fruit of the Spirit.*

> *"But the fruit of the Spirit is love, joy, peace, longsuffering, kindness, goodness, faithfulness, gentleness, self-control. Against such there is no law."* (Gal. 5:22–23)

I could hardly wait for His dynamic power to flow through me. I wanted all His magnificent glory to be seen in every area of my being. I wanted to be just like Christ and like that preacher who led me to Christ! I prayed to represent that powerful anointing with biblical indicators (read these chapters; Acts 2, Gal. 5, and Eph. 3). I wanted to share the *Good News* with everyone in the world, as I was indeed being planted by the beautiful hands of the living God (but I was not rooted yet).

> *"There are diversities of gifts, but the same Spirit. There are differences of ministries, but the same Lord. And there are diversities of activities, but it is the same God who works all in all. But the manifestation of the Spirit is given to each one for the profit of all: for to one is given the word of wisdom through the Spirit, to another the word of knowledge through the same Spirit, to another faith by the same Spirit, to another gifts of healings by the same Spirit, to another the working of miracles, to another prophecy, to another discerning of spirits, to another different kinds of tongues, to another the interpretation of tongues. But one and the same Spirit works all these things, distributing to each one individually as He wills."* (1 Cor. 12:4–11)

There was an internal God-conscience now leading and guiding me (my inner GPS – God's Powerful Spirit), upholding me, and guiding me through life. I wanted to have this spiritual satellite help me navigate through each day. Every day with Christ began to get better, and I saw His blessings and favor working!

I had a keen new awareness of the identity and divinity of Christ. I found the need to deliberately exercise my physical and spiritual senses. I was attuned to His heart, and His thoughts were becoming my thoughts. Christ's ways were becoming my ways, and His pleasures, perspective, and purpose in my life began to get brighter.

The Holy Spirit did not just lead me and tell me about the good things in my life. But He also started letting me know what disappointed Father God concerning me. He showed me my many shortcomings, failures, and unacceptable habits that did not glorify God in my body (1 Cor. 6:18–20). He told me what I needed to change and *thoroughly* work on, work through, and intentionally work out.

I had become spiritually awakened, aware, and alert to the Kingdom of God and His way of doing things and living upright (God's righteous path). Therefore, I could no longer go to certain places. There were people I could no longer hang around. I could no longer ignore situations and things I needed to correct. He wanted me to be holy as He is holy truly (1 Pet. 1:15–16).

I realized that salvation does not take the place of an apology, forgiveness, or righting the wrongs done to others (the Holy Spirit leads us into *all truth*, even the sad truth about ourselves)!

How could I walk in the light if I did not get things right (holding grudges and having an unforgiving heart is darkness)? How could I claim to be different if I lived, spoke, and acted the same? My Christian obligation is to live in the light that God has provided through Christ: *"Now you are light in the Lord. Walk as children of light"* (Eph. 5:8). I was to let my light "shine before men" (Matt. 5:16) so the whole world could see the power and love of Jesus! *"But if we walk in the light, as he is in the light, we have fellowship with one another, and the blood of Jesus, His Son, cleanses us from all sin"* (1 John 1:7).

I loved being engulfed in Him and spiritual freedom. A new way of life and a new way of thinking was my choice. Oh, what a glorious time we had together.

I felt at times as if I were on a personal planet with God, and no one was there but me. I envisioned my supreme assignment was to become an alien on Earth (instead of a Martian, I was a Christian). My task once on Earth was to convince others to receive Christ wholeheartedly. I was to teach them how to live according to the *Christian manual*, fight against the opposing forces, and keep helping more Christians rejoice in having an alien status as they lived for Christ. Then Christ would come to take us back to His *heavenly planet* to live with Him forever (because this world is not our home)! This vision helped me to understand the Christian mission and commission given by Christ more clearly.

Definitively, I had left the world and many of my old friends, so now it was time for me to connect with new people (like-minded believers) who would enhance my spiritual growth. As a result, I began to faithfully attend more church services with the intent to be taught and to serve. I started to fellowship and meet others who also *seemed* to have experienced this miraculous work. I needed people around me who were radicals for Christ and loved God wholeheartedly (naturally, I thought a church was the ultimate answer).

A short while later, I began serving and volunteering my time. Afterward I dedicated my life to working diligently in ministry. Next, I took part in prayer, Bible study, evangelism, and spiritual mentoring and counseling. I did everything I felt the Holy Spirit led me to do, as I could feel His presence, His glory, and His warmth of grace surrounding me regularly. Serving God's people was so exciting! Allowing God to use me was beyond impressive. These events surpassed my expectations and *basic* understanding. It was surreal but oh so real!

The Shock of My Life

My life renewal brought forth credulous confidence (faith), inexplicable joy, a powerful peace, sanctifying self-worth, and an unfathomable understanding of His sovereign supremacy concerning me. My heart was His, I was *all in*, and there was no turning back! Thus, my Christian life was excellent, until one day, in one instant, **everything changed** (yes, "in one instant")!

Growing up going to church as a child, I had been strictly taught to believe that church was the *House of God* and a *House of Prayer,* not man's playground. I thought the church was a holy place for ungodly people to be taught and groomed for discipleship. Where the unholy could learn to be both honorable and righteous in the sight of God. I grew up imagining that nothing wrong, evil, or wicked would or could dwell in the House of God for long. I believed that the church would attack evil like ants attacking strange bugs near their mound or bees attacking invaders. I believed that the church would come against demonic spirits as bees come against anything and anyone who stirs them up! I just knew sin could never find comfort and lodge in a power-packed place like the church! The older Saints said a church was a healing and deliverance center, a soul-saving station, or a *soul depot* for life

31

improvement (like Home Depot is for home improvement). I sincerely thought a church was where believers could learn their purpose and obtain spiritual knowledge and understanding while growing in grace. I believed the Holy Spirit led and taught people through the word of God how to effectively use their gifts, talents, and time to disseminate the power and love of God to others around the world.

I believed that church was where the lost could be found, the weak could be made strong, and the poor could learn to become rich on any level (spiritually, mentally, emotionally, physically, and economically). I knew from the scriptures that the believer's body was to share abundantly with others (not hoard it for selfish greed or worldly gain). I thought a church was where the Holy Spirit resided (both in the building and the people). I believed the church building was supposed to be a loving, spiritual residence for families, a perpetual sanctuary and shelter of safety for those needing spiritual refuge and help.

I was taught as a kid that dirty hands were not to touch the holy things of God. Unrighteous people with unclean (impure) hearts could not serve a righteous God. Was I taught wrongly? If so, why are there so many scriptures that state otherwise?

"Little children, let no one deceive you. Whoever practices righteousness is righteous, as he is righteous." (1 John 3:7)

"Blessed are the pure in heart, for they shall see God." (Matt. 5:8)

"Create in me a clean heart, O God, and renew a right spirit within me." (Ps. 51:10)

"Draw near to God, and he will draw near to you. Cleanse your hands, you sinners, and purify your hearts, you double-minded." (James 4:8)

"So, flee youthful passions and pursue righteousness, faith, love, and peace, along with those who call on the Lord from a pure heart." (2 Tim. 2:22)

"Who shall ascend the hill of the Lord? And who shall stand in his holy place? He who has clean hands and a pure heart, who does not lift up his soul to what is false and does not swear deceitfully." (Ps. 24:3–4)

"If you know that he is righteous, you may be sure that everyone who practices righteousness has been born of him." (1 John 2:29)

I thought every Christian serving in a church went to church to change their old ways, drop their bad habits, and practice a new way of living. Yes, this should occur, but unfortunately, this is not the expectation or standard in every church.

I quickly realized that I could not live off the delusion of a "happy, happy, joy, joy" Christian mentality, wherein every day would be a glorious "magic carpet" ride with Jesus.

Shark Bait

Unfortunately, I was not rooted and grounded in the word of God yet. All those years in the church, from childhood to adulthood, did not prepare or equip me to endure these spiritual attacks (it trained me to sit in a building, not at the feet of Christ). I did not take the time to learn how to discern both good and evil (Heb. 5:7–14), and it cost me greatly.

I soon found out that I was gullible, too trusting, too new to the game, and way *too saved* for my good (if there is any such thing). I was live bait for the hungry spiritual sharks who were waiting for me to step out of my secure boat of faith only to get devoured in this uncharted territory. I was out of my league, there was no safety net around, there was no turning back, and they smelled new blood in the atmosphere! Can you picture it yet? (If not, think about the movie *Jaws*.)

I entered this new arena of false fellowship, fakes, and frauds with no spiritual understanding, no armor, and no quantified training. My "new" heart was exposed to the undermining spirits of trickery (Prov. 4:23). My enthusiasm for Christ made me a prime target and a sitting duck for what was to come, but that was not the worst part! I was unguarded and ungrounded, and I had too many immature expectations coming in the door.

Proceed with Caution

No one had warned me that not everyone holding a leadership position or title in a church wanted to truly live holy to see the results of the faith that pleased God (Heb. 11:6) or become new in Christ (2 Cor. 5:17).

My walk with Christ became a daily psychological and spiritual struggle for me after unknowingly connecting with people who were not Christlike but pretended to be holy. This downfall was a personal whirlwind; this was an individual satanic thunderstorm created just for me (and yours are tailored just for you as well). This storm lasted for several months (and affected me for a few years afterwards). I was lied on, talked about, criticized, ostracized, and on top of that, I was a relatively new Christian convert. I was not new to the church settings, but I was new to church folks like these. I had been *spiritually wounded* by their fiery darts of poison (like I had never seen while I was in the world). These people barely knew my name, yet they had serious issues with the God in me!

I had received Christ in one season, and the following season I had stirred up Satan's camp (like hitting an active hornets' nest with a baseball bat). I had to run for my spiritual life! I was being attacked in every way, all because I chose Christ! How could this be? (Study every chapter in Ephesians, as it will prepare you to stand against such attacks. Also, read these other chapters for growth, maturity, and understanding: Mat.5, Luke 6, Cor. 12, 2 Tim. 3–4, John 10:15, and 1 John 3).

> *"For we do not wrestle against flesh and blood, but against the rulers, against the authorities, against the cosmic powers over this present darkness, against the spiritual forces of evil in the heavenly places."* (Eph. 6:12)

> *"Indeed, all who desire to live a godly life in Christ Jesus will be persecuted, while evil people and impostors will go on from bad to worse, deceiving and being deceived. But as for you, continue in what you have learned and have firmly believed, knowing from whom you learned it and how from childhood you have been acquainted with the sacred writings, which are able to make you wise for salvation through faith in Christ Jesus. All Scripture is breathed out by God and profitable for teaching, for reproof, for correction, and for training in righteousness, that the man of God may be complete, equipped for every good work."* (2 Tim. 3:12–17)

Unfortunately, most Christians will not understand the magnitude of these types of attacks or the forces behind them until they find themselves in the trenches fighting for their spiritual lives.

Multitudes of people in ministry today barely make it through this onslaught of spiritual attacks. Unfortunately, some must face this ferocious assault alone because of the calling on their lives. Others are overcome by a mental crisis and have never fully recovered (possibility due to operating in things they were never equipped to do; they went but were not *God*-sent). Countless others never see victory because Satan provoked their minds to quit, faint, lose heart, and backslide. Regrettably, some commit suicide after becoming overwhelmed due to mental anguish, depression, or demonic oppression. Most were void of spiritual support, sufficient biblical training, or simply lack faith in God.

Like many "babes in Christ" (new, born-again believers or new Christian converts), I knew much of nothing about church matters. I knew less about what is often called *church hurt* (fully detailed in Book 3) when I began serving in ministry more than twenty years ago. Therefore, I was ill-equipped and unprepared when these unexpected things beyond my understanding and control started happening.

Satan began to up his antics by using cunning, deceitful, and manipulative demonic spirits against me (in the form of illegitimate Christians; you will read more about them in this book and those to follow in this series). I had countless encounters and sometimes exhaustingly debilitating moments of constant spiritual battles within the church walls. I had to relentlessly face and confront fierce, strong, dark, and evil people. I was not spiritually equipped or mentally prepared to fight against these weapons that had been fashioned against me in the form of church people.

Satan strategically planned to wage war against me from day one with every step I made toward drawing closer to God through Christ. I chose Christ over everything! It seemed as if all the powers of Hell broke loose and vehemently came for me with a vengeance! I felt like Satan's bomb attacks had spiritually obliterated my faith and separated me from God's safety net.

Allowing the Lord Jesus Christ to keep my mind during these times was a significant feat in itself. I wanted to run far away, and on occasion, I wanted to die! I could barely focus on Him anymore or His written word. This despair was due to the demonically driven, power-packed punches and fiery arrows and torpedoes (not just darts) that kept coming my way. They were coming from "Christians"; I looked up to these very people! I felt useless, dumb, and numb at the same time. I was crushed and devastated!

Can you believe that I wanted to fade away from this earth one season shortly after salvation? Can you believe the devil had me thinking that the Lord had left me in the middle of those shark-infested waters to die? He had me convinced that God could not be trusted (but that was a lie)!

I Did Not Know

I was oblivious to what was happening to me after being blindsided and ambushed by Hell's angels disguised as Saints (within the "House of God," no less). These Christlike pretenders caused me considerable spiritual distress, mental agony, and soul-wrenching torment. I was ignorant and unaware! Who knew that the simple and innocent act of giving my life to Christ could cause so much drama?

[The lukewarm, half-hearted, evil-spirited, unloving, ungodly, over-religious, self-righteous churchgoers cause 98 percent of the mayhem in Christian organizations.]

I did not know that churchgoers felt it was okay and justifiable to set aside their relationship with Christ (or, as some people say, "put down their religion") to validate any ungodly behavior that they plan to do or say. I did not know that many churchgoers are still doing almost any- and everything they want to do (outside of the word of God) without genuine remorse or repentance, and even serve as if their hearts and hands are clean (Gal. 6:1–6, Heb. 4:16).

I did not know churchgoers behave like childish preschool children by bickering, biting, squealing, and throwing tantrums. I did not realize that some churchgoers will do just about anything to be seen and heard or get any attention (even negative attention). I did not know that many senior churchgoers could be worse than baby Christians (some are mean-spirited bullies with a negative influence over the congregation). I honestly never imagined that some churchgoers could be so petty, overly sensitive, unforgiving, sour, and extremely bitter after being *saved* for many years. There are multitudes of churchgoers who have no spiritual desire to grow or do better, and they remain the same from one year to the next (some for decades or even to death, or from time to eternity).

How could these church folks act as if they had never heard the spoken Word of God (before, during, or after salvation)? How could they fraudulently defend their actions to justify themselves and cause further offense to others? Were they truly saved? Their hearts and minds were still in the world. They still acted like the devil after receiving Christ, uniting with a ministry, getting baptized, and being filled with the precious Holy Spirit (and some with the evidence of speaking in tongues)! They did not desire to go from glory to glory. They failed to graduate from the "churchgoer" level to attain "Christlike" status. They continued to be cruel and wickedly hurt others because they are spiritually dysfunctional, deceived and in denial. They will never hear "well done", but they will hear "I knew you not" if they have not changed (please study Mat. 25:1–46 and Mat. 7: 21–23)! I was uninformed, misinformed, and closed-minded concerning those who *supposedly* were walking in the ways of God (especially those in leadership). Many seldom displayed a proper knowledge of God's love or character. They also did not take the life, death, and resurrection of Christ seriously enough to be examples of godliness for people like me. Theoretically, most should have been more mature in the word before taking on any ministry position or leading anybody in any way.

I did not know this could happen (and still happens) when Christians become prideful. The word of God then becomes distorted in their understanding (twisted by Satan), and they resist the leading of the Holy Spirit. Their hearts wax cold, their eyes are blinded, and their ears go deaf to what is biblically sound and correct. They abort the word to justify their actions, just as many priests and religious leaders did concerning Stephen in Acts chapters 6 and 7. Many unregenerate Christians live as if they never knew Christ. They can be so callous, insensitive, reckless, and outright cruel, with flagrant disregard for what is biblically written. They become ministry saboteurs!

Looking at what I have gained, the worst part (or the best part) was that I soon understood that ungodly and evil spirits could comfortably dwell in a powerless and deceived church and in powerless and deceived people. Some of these evil spirits are *allowed* to camp out. Some of these spirits are just waiting for you to arrive. Some are ancient or generational spirits; they have been there for a long time. Others are familiar spirits; they act like loving family, until they get jealous (or envious) of you, then they toss you in a deep, dry pit (read about Joseph in Genesis chapters 37–50)!

These unholy churchgoers actually lead people, take part in worship, teach Bible study, and will have friendly fellowships with you, all before trying to kill you spiritually (as Judas did with Jesus—see Matthew chapters 26 and 27, and Luke chapter 22). These people can be both male or female, of any color and any age. If allowed, those same satanic spirits can readily attach themselves to the leaders and the church's lay members who are ill-equipped, unprepared, and unaware. When this happens, powerless church services will continue as usual.

Why, Why, Why?

A short season after my miraculous change, conversion, and encounter with God, I was ready to quit the ministry! Here I was, high on Christ one moment, then deliberately crushed, hurt, stunned, and bewildered the next moment! How could this be? How did Satan find a way to crash my party with Christ and interrupt my divine fellowship with the Spirit of God?

I had so many plaguing questions, such as: Why was I attacked while trying to do the will of God? Why were the scales tilted in the devil's favor against me? Why were Christians so mean and evil to each other for no good reason? Why were church leaders blind to what those under their leadership were doing (especially their own family and friends)? Why could other people not see how much help the "baby" Saints needed? Why were some members treated better than others? How could those with no anointing lead? Why were people so disengaging and careless with their actions, attitudes, and words? Why were there so many ungodly things named among the people of God? Why were people so pretentious? Why were the older Saints and five-fold ministry gifts not teaching, helping, or equipping the younger generation to grow and mature in grace and in the knowledge of Christ (2 Pet. 3:18)? Why do they look down on them and talk badly about them? Where was the Church Christ spoke of in Matthew chapter 16? Why was the Holy Spirit not teaching the adults how to behave at home and in the House of the Lord? Where was the love of God? *Where was God, and why was He not intervening?* These were some of the many unanswered questions that taunted my mind. I had no peace, no help, no joy, no answers, and I had nowhere to go!

God does not want another person in His divine family of sons (or daughters) to be as ill-prepared for this type of "church" as I was. I sincerely aim to do so if I can help prevent anyone else from being sorely wounded by the *War Within the Walls, Internal Persecution* (another book in this series). The gates of Hell will not prevail against **real Christians/Christ-followers** (the true Church) that Christ is coming back for, not the imposters.

The Aftershock

I never denounced or cursed God, but I was angry, broken, and deeply discouraged about the internal persecution that was openly going on. I knew as a Christ-follower that I was to take on the world for Christ, but I did not realize that I had to take on the church! I was internally condemning Him for everything I was going through, and I did not want to acknowledge Him or His Son! Yes, while I was going through church hurt, *I was angry at God*!

Soon after, I started a downward spiral into depression, self-pity, and powerlessness. Post-Traumatic Church Hurt (PTCH) caused me to withdraw. I did not want to participate in many church services or affiliated church events, nor did I want to be around or hear from "churchy" people. I even began to backslide from reading the word of God. I did not want to trust or hear my Father's voice or any church subject anymore (all because of the incapacitating agony the Church represented to me). I was miserable, I was mad, and I was weak in every way!

As time went on, I would reluctantly commune with God. I rarely prayed in the Spirit or meditated on the word; instead, I reflected on my hurt and pain. When I did pray (from time to time), the prayers had no sincerity in my heart. I would listen to Christian songs and sing, but not with the joy I once had. I would read the scriptures, but not with any purpose for understanding. I would go to different churches at times, but my heart was still heavy and my spirit was sorely vexed. My body would be there, but my mind was elsewhere. I was so spiritually numb that I went through the motions and checked the religious boxes (as countless people do in every church service).

There were times I considered joining a new church, but the reasons I should not join would flood over my cognizance at each visit to remain an observant visitor. The entire church experience became sort of comical and ridiculous after a while. I felt that God and church were a joke! I would sit there and feel absolutely nothing; I heard nothing useful, and the funny part was no one even noticed me.

[If there is no one in your church effectively perceiving and adequately ministering to spiritual trauma, downcast people, and weeping souls, it may be due to faulty leadership, fear, and lack of good teaching.]

Like so many today, I felt lost in a place where I found Christ (the church). I felt hopeless where hope was supposed to be found. I was perplexed and somewhat alienated from the church I attended and isolated from the world I had recently left behind. I was stuck between two worlds and did not want to be in either one of them. I still had so many questions, burdensome concerns, a lot of fears, countless tears, yet no one to turn to and no one to talk to about anything.

I was grieving from the hurt, and later I began to lament, because supposedly there were a few "super-spiritual seasoned saints" (S4s) in my church, yet no one was spiritual enough to reach out to me. No one noticed my countenance or discerned the spirit of heaviness weighing me down. This lack of care outraged me even more than the initial treatment! I was a Christian, and they were Christians of a higher caliber, so why weren't their spiritual gifts kicking in to help me? I soon found out that many Christian S4s were powerfully powerless! They would talk strong but left me on the ministry battlefield to spiritually fend for myself as I emotionally bled to death at the hands of those who ran me into the wilderness to die *alone*!

During this dark and bleak time in the dismal drylands of my Christian life, no one came to my aid. No one could save me. There was no one around to understand, console, or comfort me genuinely. It seemed as if no one could even hear or see me during this season, nor could they perceive the painful barrenness I was going through by myself!

Christ no longer held first place in my heart, and I was shattered into a million pieces. Sadly, my pain and bitterness were what I woke up to daily and slept with nightly. I had no real rest and no real zeal for the things of God. I had no inner peace or spiritual direction during these times. I was a spiritual POW (prisoner of war) in my soul; I suffered from severe PTCH (Post-Traumatic Church Hurt).

After the Aftershock

There is no worse feeling than being intentionally hurt and rejected by those who you would sincerely think to have (or should have) your best interest at heart. My confidence in God was all but gone. In this season, I felt abandoned by God and His people, and it was an unthinkable aftershock to my soul.

Then came the torture! Satan made me question my faith in God by presenting false imaginations, evil thoughts, and questions, such as: How does a good God let horrible things happen to innocent people like you? Is any of this faith stuff real? Is it worth the trouble just to get to heaven? You never went through things this bad when you were in the world. How could God leave you feeling so overwhelmed, troubled, and abandoned? All you wanted to do is be of service to Him, and this is your thanks? All Christians are fakes! He does not love you! If God loved you, He would have prevented this pain!

I had no fight left in me, and these thoughts began to mount daily (relentlessly at times). I went from anger to becoming furious with God (on the inside). I contended with a strong inner voice shouting for revenge and demanding someone pay for my pain (explained in chapter 6). I did not know what to do or believe anymore.

> *"Casting down imaginations, and every high thing that exalted itself against the knowledge of God, and bringing into captivity every thought to the obedience of Christ; And having in a readiness to revenge all disobedience, when your obedience is fulfilled."* (2 Cor. 10:5–6)

Total Surrender, Again

Months after my spiritual deficit, I was still sorely wounded, wallowing in deep spiritual sorrow and depression. I needed intense soul therapy and church rehabilitation. I was so baffled and bitter concerning God's "so-called" servants. Yet I still did not know or understand the root cause of the problem. Nor did I know who to trust, where I belonged, or what to think about my faith. I was profusely annoyed with *those people*, and I stopped wanting to spend time with God altogether.

The church body was not the abuser, but a few members of the church were spiritually abusive, harmful, and highly insensitive. The church body (as a whole) was not bad, but those few bad apples in that bunch were filled with snakes, not worms. The absence of the Holy Spirit in their lives affected my growth as a new Christian and as a new member.

Introspective

I did not even notice how lukewarm I had become. I did not look to Jesus as the Author and the Finisher of my faith. I had intentionally tucked my true feelings away from God (as if I could). I locked and blocked Him out of my life. I tried to make Him inaccessible to my emotions (and somewhat inaccessible to me). I ignored His tender knocks on the door of my heart; He could not reveal His plan to heal me, and I did not care anymore! I refused to continue the wonderful communion and divine fellowship (*koinonia*) we once shared. I quit trusting the process, the word, and His power. I was not sinning in the world, but my thoughts, anger, and hardened heart were sinful enough!

I had drifted so far away from God, yet there was still something drawing me back to Him (I know it was the Holy Spirit). Somehow I started having more reminiscent thoughts about the good times we shared (before the spiritual exile). I would often find myself daydreaming and mentally wishing for those times of intimate fellowship to return.

Then one day, I heard the Spirit say "REJOICE"! Rejoice? How, when there is so much craziness going on in my life? What is there to be joyful about right now?

The Steps Forward

After wallowing in sorrow, I finally yielded, and took the first steps to draw closer to the God I once adored (James 4:7-8). I decided to dust off my Bible and flipped through it for some highlighted scriptures to read. The first scripture I came across was Philippians 4:4, ***"Rejoice in the Lord always; again, I will say, rejoice."*** Well, that made me laugh! Out of the thousands of verses I could have landed on, the first one I had read in almost a year says "rejoice"? God definitely has a sense of humor! I let Him humor me further, and I kept reading to see where He would lead me (Phil. 4:5-9).

> *"Let your reasonableness be known to everyone. The Lord is at hand; do not be anxious about anything, but in everything by prayer and supplication with thanksgiving, let your requests be made known to God. And the peace of God, which surpasses all understanding, will guard your hearts and your minds in*

Christ Jesus. Finally, brothers, whatever is true, whatever is honorable, whatever is just, whatever is pure, whatever is lovely, whatever is commendable, if there is any excellence, if there is anything worthy of praise, think about these things. What you have learned and received and heard and seen in me—practice these things, and the God of peace will be with you." (Phil. 4:5-9, Amp.)

Instantly, all those prior glorious and beautiful past experiences with God were worthy of praise and gave me peace! I smiled with tears rolling down my face, took a deep breath, and then released it all as I exhaled the pain. I perceived this was about to go somewhere unexpected; I knew a change had finally come! An airy feeling came into my heart, and I was assured that I was still a child of God and that He still loved me unconditionally.

I knew if I remained paralyzed by those hurtful and mean people, I would eventually fall apart. I did not want to leave the loving arch of safety provided by the Lord. If I did not choose to step forward out of my pit of pain into His inviting comfort, I would remain in this depressive and hopeless state (which was far from living). I quickly understood that my state would worsen if I did not let God handle this mess *now*.

Self-Honesty

There were many times I felt sad for abrogating Christ from His (now permanent) throne of Lordship in my life. I was hesitant at first, but I was ready to get right in His presence. I asked the Holy Spirit to begin to minister to me and teach me how to rise above all the heartache (and those who caused it). I was afraid to trust the process and take the necessary steps forward, but I needed Jesus to help my unbelief (Mark 9:14–25). I was hurting so badly! I was sad, confused, tired, and desperate for a change. I needed help, I needed power, and I needed prayer! I wanted my spirit and soul to be cleansed from this seemingly endless depression.

Ultimately, I prayed with everything in me, then the labor and birthing process of total restoration began. There were several things I had to get rooted in my heart before moving forward, and the first thing was to **willingly repent**. I sat at the edge of my bed with remorseful sorrow, I asked the God to forgive every thought, and every known and unknown sin I had committed against Him.

I felt uncomfortable because I could not find the right words to pray or say, but I did not want to remain stuck in the pit of bitter sullenness. I did not want my life to persist in this miserable existence. I did not want to be a self-righteous, angry, unforgiving, prideful, negative, excuse-making, ignorant backslider who would always blame others for why I was not going to church or developing a stronger relationship with Christ. I did not want evil to be victorious over me! I needed to call out to God for strength! So, I told Him all those things straight from my heart. Honestly, I was still somewhat upset at Him, but I wanted to see where this would lead, so I threw my cares at the feet of Jesus (James 5:7–9).

Next, I opened my heart and surrendered to the *Truth* of God's love.

As I uttered the name of **Jesus**, tears began to fall. I prayed a few more words, then I began to cry. I got down on my knees to worship and cried even more. I wept deeply to the point where everything inside of me felt like a river wall breaking! Suddenly, the pain, grief, despair, anger, bitterness, sadness, regrets, aches, rage, resentment, desolation, and fear welded in my heart and flooded my soul all at once! My crying soon turned into wailing, and there was a groaning coming from deep within. I cried out for help, and like a good Father, my God came to my rescue (Ps. 40:13–17, 71:4; 2 Tim. 4:16–18)!

The worship began, and the tears flowed for more than an hour. My soul was emptying, and my spirit was being revived. There was a massive amount of internal soul pressure released as God's Spirit moved upon me. All the heaviness soon dissipated, and I was soon sprawled on the floor with no more words to say besides *"Thank You, Lord,"* over and over again!

After much travail, I had finally broken through! I felt free; I was finally free! For the first time in almost a year, I could feel again! I was alive! The numbness was gone. His goodness was moving powerfully within me and filling the empty places with joy. It was the Spirit of the living God! I began to dance in His presence! No music, just the sweet sound of peace filling my heart once again! Hallelujah!

A New Revelation of the Cross

After my soulful lament, the blinders were immediately removed. The Spirit of God came in and dealt with me and my grief. I then understood that Christ came to lay down His life for the very thing I endured. He came to heal the brokenhearted. He did it for me (Luke 4:18)!

Jesus was beaten, tortured, and tormented on the Cross to save me from the residual effects of spiritual beatdowns, torture, and torment. He also came to restore my soul after suffering persecution here on Earth (Ps. 23:3). Yeshua (Hebrew name) endured the Cross and despised the shame to build me up when life tears me down (Heb. 12:1–2)! Jesus came to repair the breaches in my life. He came to pull down satanic strongholds, to break every debilitating chain and curse. The Son of God came to destroy every ungodly yoke and remove my worldly burdens (Isa. 10:27). Jesus came to give me the peace that passes all understanding! He came to provide me with abundant life above what the devil tried to steal, kill, and destroy in me (John 10:10)! My Savior came to deliver me from evil, so I would fear no evil; faith dominates fear (Ps. 23:4, Matt. 6:13, 2 Tim. 1:7). He came to comfort. intercede, advocate, counsel, encourage, and strengthen by His Sprit (John 14:26, Rom. 8:26-30, 2 Cor. 1:3)! He came to give me beauty for ashes, gladness instead of sorrow, and sweet praise over a bitter and dry spirit (Isa. 61:3)! He came to take the veil away and set this captive free (John 8:36, 2 Cor. 3:17)!

> *"Surely, he has borne our griefs and carried our sorrows; yet we esteemed him stricken, smitten by God and afflicted. But he was wounded for our transgressions; he was crushed for our iniquities; upon him was the chastisement that brought us peace, and with his stripes, we are healed. All we like sheep have gone astray; we have turned every one to his own way, and the LORD has laid on him the iniquity of us all."* (Isa. 53:3–6)

> *"The Spirit of the Lord God is upon me, because the Lord has anointed me to bring good news to the poor; He has sent me to bind up the brokenhearted, to proclaim liberty to the captives, and the opening of the prison to those who are bound; to proclaim the year of the Lord's favor, and the day of vengeance of our God; to comfort all who mourn; to grant to those who mourn in Zion— to give them a beautiful headdress instead of ashes, the oil of gladness instead of mourning, the garment of praise instead of a faint spirit; that they may be called oaks of righteousness, the planting of the Lord, that he may be glorified."* (Isa. 61:1–3)

Always There

Through it all, my heavenly Father was there with me. Even when I drifted, He was there. He has always been there and will always be with me (Heb. 13:5–6). I did not fully understand the magnitude of His commitment during my hard times until I read Isaiah 43:2. Then that scripture became personal for my situation. Just as those words gave the Israelites hope during their Babylonian struggles, those words also resounded in my spirit. He is the same God today, and His word still stands.

> *"When you pass through the waters, I will be with you, and through the rivers, they will not overwhelm you. When you walk through the fire, you will not be burned or scorched, nor will the flame kindle upon you."* (Isa. 43:2)

He never rejected me; He was there to keep me sane! He was there protecting me from the evildoers and saving me from self-destruction. He was walking me through the rough and stormy sea. He was taking me *through* the fiery trials!

I had briefly turned my back on the Lord's love, yet He kept turning His heart toward me! Jesus did not ignore my questions; He waited for me to seek Him for answers (Matt. 7:7–8, 6:33). My Savior did not disregard my pain or previous cries for help. He was reaching down, but I was not reaching up for His help. Through it all, my Lord saw something in me that I never knew was there, and He received me with open arms.

Called & Chosen

God's plan and calling on my life did not change because of what I had gone through. He still called me (and that will never change). He still wanted me as His daughter (and I desired to please Him). He had a specific use for me (and I wanted to be a vessel of honor, fit for His glorious use). He still believed in me (and I wanted so badly to be believed in again). I had to allow Him to restore my soul, lead me back to the path of righteousness for *His* namesake, anoint my head with fresh oil, and abundantly take care of me in the presence of my enemies as He blesses me to be a blessing (Ps. 23). I had to give my Shepherd my all!

I could not let those bad apples, with bad seeds and rotting roots, affect my harvest and stop me from harvesting souls for His Kingdom! I had to heal completely (the importance of healing God's way is thoroughly explained more in book two of this series). I had to unreservedly receive that truth of my heavenly Father's love for me, and all that entails.

Even though I was a wreck at the time, the word and power of God saved me. I was saved by grace through faith from Hell, and then I was saved from the hands of the enemy because God loved me! My heavenly

Father never gave up on me because He loved me! Yahweh saw beyond my weaknesses and gave me strength. Through the agony and the defeat, through it all, He loved me! Thank you, Lord, for unconditional love! I bless and praise Your Holy name!

Know that He will never give up on you and that He loves you too!

Read Hebrews 13:5, 1 John 4:18, and 2 John 4:16 for more assurance. Thank you, Lord, for unconditional love! I bless and praise Your Holy name for loving us so much!

The Calling

I thanked God for being so gracious toward me and coming to my rescue (once again). I began to weep, as there was such an overwhelming presence of the Holy Spirit in my room. A calm and a relaxing peace came over me; I heard the Holy Spirit speak on the inside: ***"Be encouraged, the trials of faith will strengthen you to help others overcome their hurt and hopelessness, as you heal."*** I was relieved to hear His voice again. I tried to disregard the message, hoping my crying would make me forget because I was apprehensive and did not want to help anyone.

During that week, I began to wholeheartedly worship and praise God, when I heard Him speak again, *"Be encouraged, the trials of faith will strengthen you to help others overcome their hurt as they heal. Get up; you have Kingdom work to do!"* I began to pray for wisdom and understanding. I was led to this scripture in Luke 22:31–32, where Jesus says to Peter, ***"Simon, Simon! Indeed, Satan has asked for you, that he may sift you as wheat. But I have prayed for you, that your faith should not fail; and when you have returned to Me (been converted), strengthen your brethren."***

Peter had a warning from Jesus; he was told that the enemy was coming for him. Unfortunately, out of pride and misjudgment concerning his faith level, He did not comprehend this prediction. His faith faltered at a crucial time as a follower of Christ. Like Peter, I could not see what was to come or completely understand what was being said to me at the time. Unlike Peter, I had no one training or teaching me in these matters at the time. I did not know (or I had forgotten) that Jesus was always praying for me until I read Hebrews 7:25, *"Therefore He is also able to save to the uttermost those who come to God through Him since He always lives to make intercession (intervention and prayerful mediation) for them."*

What I had gone through was already integrated into His divine plan for my good and His glory (Rom. 8:28). Then it hit me! Even though my faith waivered for a short period, the prayers of Christ kept me. My faith did not completely fail. It waivered because circumstances made me doubt, but my faith did not die! Jesus was still praying for me (study John chapter 17 and Romans chapter 8). He knew this was necessary for my making because I too would need to go back (like Peter) and strengthen my brothers and sisters in Christ one day. The Lord knew my heart and knew that I sincerely needed Him. He knew this evil would work for my good (as it did for Joseph in Genesis chapters 37–50 and many others in the Bible, such as is written in 1 Peter 3:8–17).

I had to go all out, give it all up, start all over again with Christ, and walk into a place of true discipleship despite the agony. Amid the excruciating aches and desolation, I still wanted to be a virtuous Christian, a respectable woman of God, and a triumphant success in Kingdom building. I had to become adequately qualified in disregarding the pain and not rehearsing my woes.

Therefore, God needed to re-lay the foundation and reinforce it to make it unmovable, unbreakable, effective, and firmly secure in Him. This downfall was intentionally allowed to reveal my purpose in God and Christ's purpose for going to the Cross on my behalf. The trial was allowed so I could see the God of my salvation walk me through the waters without drowning or dying. Persecution was allowed to show me where I was deficient in my faith. It allowed me to reveal areas that needed fortified, repaired, replaced, and renewed before another attack arose. The time in the furnace helped me spiritually. I now understand what the enemy of my soul wanted to do to me and those who lack spiritual knowledge in the face of adversity. The pain was allowed to teach me how to guard my heart and discern the hearts of men and women before making spiritual or natural (flesh-driven) connections. My *foundation of faith* was not concrete or strong enough to endure much of anything before the attacks, so this was necessary *for me*.

Forgiving Those People

Foolishly, I thought everyone was authentically desiring to be better, do better, and wanted to help others do the same. I innocently did not consider that some were pretending to be more advanced than they actually were. They were attending church, ministering to people, and serving God with the attitude and heart of Satan! I unwillingly witnessed and soon became a target and a victim of the vast amount of hypocrisy, judgment, jealousy, criticism, and sometimes straight-out hatred from these imposters!

My misconception was that those leaders professing salvation left their worldly ways, speech, and past lifestyles. I presumed everyone serving was joyfully in awe of His impact in their lives to such a degree that their attitudes reflected His glory, and their encounter with Christ demanded permanent change. I just knew there would be an overflow of real love, welcoming hearts, and forgiving spirits in the church, especially from those who had titles and held *important* positions. I assumed that everyone in the church had seen enough, been through enough, and had enough of their sinful ways, wicked lifestyles, and pointless relationships. I thought all leading Christians wanted to "taste and see that the Lord is good" (Ps. 34:8). (Read all of Psalm 34.) I thought the church was where wisdom, age, and spiritual maturity went together (but what was I thinking?).

For this reason, we should never view soul-ministry as a tragic mistake or as a tactless, spiteful, useless, and troublesome burden. Through the love and grace of God, it can be an ongoing, delightful, wondrous joyous, and exciting experience if you walk in the Spirit and develop into your rightful place in God through Christ Jesus (believe me; it is possible)! Forgive so that you will be forgiven (Matt. 6:14, Luke 11:4).

Forgive so you can heal and recover. Forgive and take your life back. Forgive for you, your growth, your future, and for your peace of mind. Forgive and turn that pain into power. Forgive and live!

Forgiving can be the hardest thing for a person who is hurting to do. It is an active response to deciding to grow in Christ beyond the wrong that has transpired. It has been referred to in poetry as being divine. Forgiveness is integral to the Christian religion, as believers are supposed to forgive each other as God forgives us. It is not always easy. It can be painfully difficult to put forth the effort to move past a wrong committed upon you, but it is direly necessary for healing.

The Bible speaks much about the need for forgiveness.

> *"Be kind to one another, tenderhearted, forgiving one another, as God in Christ forgave you."* (Eph. 4:32)

> *"If we confess our sins, He is faithful and just and will forgive us our sins and purify us from all unrighteousness."* (1 John 1:9)

> *"Bear with each other and forgive one another if any of you has a grievance against someone. Forgive as the Lord forgave you."* (Col. 3:13)

"For if you forgive other people when they sin against you, your heavenly Father will also forgive you. But if you do not forgive others their sins, your Father will not forgive your sins." (Matt. 6:14–15)

"Then Peter came to Jesus and asked, 'Lord, how many times shall I forgive my brother when he sins against me? Up to seven times?' Jesus answered, 'I tell you, not seven times, but seventy-seven times.'" (Matt. 18:21–22)

"Do not judge, and you will not be judged. Do not condemn, and you will not be condemned. Forgive, and you will be forgiven." (Luke 6:37)

Outlet for Pain

Following my spiritual restoration to God, I needed to get back to ministry. I began to chronicle my hurt, the pitfalls, my thoughts, and the revelations from God. As the Holy Spirit would speak, I would write, meditate, study, and apply what I was reading. He told me to be equipped, alert, and ready for whatever the enemy may try! He vividly showed me the causes of "church hurt," the people being used, and what I missed and overlooked the first time (because the first time was not the last time, but I am better prepared and utterly equipped to handle it throughout ministry). He showed me through scripture how important the Body of Christ was as a unit and why **real ministry** needs to be restored, taught, and adhered to, not the fleshly, self-seeking performance ministry we see in some places today.

I began to have *honest* conversations with others about how I was *healing* from "church hurt." I started not to discuss how I felt about the church as a whole but the entire process. I opened up about how I was led into the healing and moving forward in my journey to here (this area is where so many are stuck in bitterness and unforgiveness, which often leads to disease, which leads to sickness, which leads to premature death, and it is all a plot from Satan).

Once my holy fire had been re-ignited, I began to discover that my agony would surely help others regain faith, hope, and love in the spiritual nuisances that were causing them misery, complacency, and stagnant growth. I focused on helping others avoid the "ministry traps" that so many unsuspecting Christians (and non-Christians) have unwillingly fallen into outside and inside the walls of the gathering place for spiritual fellowship.

Instead of spouting venom like an angry snake, I focused on my growth. I did not need to tear down the people responsible for my pain to explain the reason, source, and seasons. I needed to concentrate on the new revelations I was receiving. I discussed how I meditated and cried out to God for help. I explained how I had to examine my heart, my faith, and my expectations. I was (and still am) the one who needed to produce more fruit. I was chosen to become more Christlike and finish strong!

I had to obey God, regardless of the hurt or the sacrifice required. I had to choose the wisest choice and stand up, become more robust in His strength, be better than before and more spiritually knowledgeable than ever: *"Behold, I send you forth as sheep in the midst of wolves: be therefore wise as serpents, and harmless as doves"* (Matt. 10:16). I had to choose to grow up and overcome the pain. I had to make the right decision and learn to help others, God's way. **I had to discover how to rise above the foolishness so I could see things as God does.** I had to learn to flourish and thrive while allowing God to make the hurt work in my favor. I had chosen to use what I call "church manure" (the yucky residue left by church hurt should be used as fertilizer for growth, not nasty messiness) to give me the spiritual nourishment needed to become a robust *fruit-bearing tree of life*. I wanted to grow, mature, and develop into a decent, virtuous, and upright vessel for Christ.

I decided to choose life! I decided to let it all go and forgive! I chose to win! **I decided to go back to church!** I chose to be an integral part of the Body of Christ. I decided to be a solution maker and not a trouble-maker. I decided to be the difference while making a difference because nothing changes until something changes! I allowed God to make my life an ongoing assignment.

A Season to Self-Evaluate and Heal

There is a process of palliative care for your heart, and it is an essential undertaking to heal properly from the root up.

I was in a severe car accident in 2006, wherein the SUV that I was in was struck on the passenger side where I was sitting. We never saw the car coming, nor was I prepared for the accident or the effects subsequently. The impact was so terrible that it flipped the SUV two or three times across to the other side of the road. The windows were broken out, the airbags deployed, the seats were broken, the tires blew out, the vehicle was a total loss. The police, ambulance, and news crews came out, and we were off to the hospital.

It was a miracle that we were alive! The officer who came to the hospital to take the report said he had seen fewer damaged vehicle accidents wherein no one involved walked away. He was not expecting us to be up and laughing without any significant bruises or bleeding, but there we were in emergency triage, laughing and praising the Lord!

After a couple of hours in the hospital, I did not feel or think much was physically wrong because I felt fine, but time told a different story.

I was out of work for several weeks, and I could not stand, sit, or lay down for long periods without significant pain. Nothing worked, and every movement hurt. There was nothing I could do but pray and trust God through the process.

I began to heal through much prayer, many doctor's visits, shedding some pounds, and carefully moving from place to place. So I began to ease back into work and a "normal" way of life.

A Right and a Wrong Way to Heal

Over a month had passed, and all seemed well, so I went to what I had hoped was my last doctor's visit for a while. At the visit, I had an upper-body movement and motion assessment, along with another X-ray. While waiting in my room for the results, the doctor came in with the report; he said, "There is good news, and there is bad news. The good news is, you are healing; the bad news is, you are healing the wrong way."

When he told me that, I was puzzled and perplexed, and I asked, "How am I healing wrongly?" He responded, "Because you were hit on the right side, the accident seemed to have shifted your spine a little to the left side. Your spine is healing to the left, and that is wrong because **you are not healing in the right place.**"

He told me that he would have to rework my spine and *attempt* to get it back to its normal position through gentle realignment, therapy, and proper back exercises. If that did not work, it would require major surgery. The doctor explained that even though I was feeling better, the effects and side effects from the accident could be more devastating and possibly debilitating in the years to come. In time, if (unknowingly) something *triggers* the muscles and nerves in that area, I could have significantly painful flare-ups while doing everyday activities.

Indeed, this was a grueling process, and correcting the problem took more time than I expected. The latter effects seemed far worse than the original pain I experienced right after the accident. It did not seem worth it at the time, but thankfully and prayerfully, the pain lessened, and after a few more months of visits, corrections, treatment, and checkups, I finally began to heal properly, and it felt good! That is when I realized that there were two ways to physically heal (the right way and the wrong way), and it is the same with spiritual hurt.

We cannot spiritually heal the right way in the wrong place.

Soul Healing (Mind, Will, Emotions)

After being hurt, I became spiritually proficient in three primary and profound areas of my life. The first triumph was genuinely operating in **unconditional love**, *no matter who, no matter what, no matter why*! The second triumph was **forgiveness**. The third triumph is to be **skilled in staying healed** (free to move forward in AGAPE love and truth, read 1 John 2). All three areas fitly complement and rely on the other. No love, no forgiveness. No forgiveness, no healing. No healing, no growth. No growth, no life. Either I received total healing from Christ, or die separated from the work of the Cross.

> *"Who is wise and understanding among you? Let him show by good conduct! that his works are done in the meekness of wisdom. But if you have bitter envy and self-seeking in your hearts, do not boast and lie against the truth. This wisdom does not descend from above but is earthly, sensual, demonic. For where envy self-seeking exist, confusion and every evil thing are there. But the wisdom that is from above is first pure, then peaceable, gentle, willing to yield, full of mercy and*

good fruits, without partiality and without hypocrisy. Now the fruit of righteousness is sown in peace by those who make peace." (James 3:13–18)

The Holy Spirit had to unction me to stop and take a moment to evaluate myself, my spiritual life, and what I was willing to become for the sake of proving a point. He revealed that instead of desperately striving to grow and mature into a godly young woman (grown, mature, and godly do not always go hand-in-hand), I was willing to allow myself to become a powerless puppet of Satan. I was chosen to be different, set apart, and deemed fit for the Master's use, not a mascot for messy mayhem.

We, as Christians, rarely take responsibility or accountability for the things we have control over. Often we blame God for the things we have allowed. We inaccurately accuse Him of causing the issues that correspond to what we chose to do. We charge Him for the things our duplicitous actions have caused. We will not recognize or accept it when it is our fault, and we need to change. We should never blame God for any of our problems because He has all of the solutions, and if we would stick to Philippians 4:8, we would most likely get over things quicker and with a much better attitude.

"Finally, brethren, whatsoever things are true, whatsoever things [are] honest, whatsoever things [are] just, whatsoever things [are] pure, whatsoever things [are] lovely, whatsoever things [are] of good report; if [there be] any virtue, and if [there be] any praise, think on these things" (Phil. 4:8, Amp).

I should not have allowed it to go as deep as it did, and it was my choice, so God allowed what I was willing to allow. However, when I was ready to be free, He allowed for my freedom, growth, and escape from emotional bondage. I had to take responsibility for my spiritual immaturity and gullible ways of thinking, and not continue to point the finger at others. I had to *grow up*, get a thicker skin, heal, and stop reacting fearfully to every adverse action, and take a stand! I had to face some of my giants with fasting and prayer. I had to face some with a slingshot and a stone, but I had to confront all my giants with a holy boldness that was firmly rooted and grounded in truth.

Things would have been different if I had just prayed, waited, and trusted God for His wise and timely answers earlier. If I had permitted the Spirit of God to comfort me in my time of anguish and heartache, things would have changed. If I had accepted the wealth of peace that Christ was offering me amid my spiritual tumult, things would not have gone this far.

Spiritual wisdom from the Holy Spirit showed me how my Heavenly Father viewed my circumstance and pain, and it was different from my personal view. I wanted to know how God could allow me to be hurt, and He wanted me to know that the hurt was not His fault, but He would help me to use that hurt for His glory by turning it into a victory story. I wanted to know how this hurt was a part of His perfect will for my life; He let me know that those bad situations would help to mature me in His love.

Blame never wins a battle; "blame is shame acting out of fear." I should have taken more spiritual responsibility and sought godly wisdom, insight, and understanding at the onset of the conflict. Even though I did not start the fight, I should have found out how to win it! I needed to get my life back and realize that conflict resolution was available for me (and it is also open to all who may desire to win, win, and win again)!

Now I had to make sure I did not add or aid in the toxic and acidic nature that so readily presents itself when we are frustrated, upset, and distracted from the purpose (as being upset is a setup for God or Satan to win). I had to want a better mindset. I had to choose my conversations and social circle ever so wisely this time. Instead of making useless excuses and making everything about me or blaming others, I made a conscious effort to heed the guidance of the Holy Spirit. I had to decide to do what I knew was right through Christ. I also chose not to remain emotionally damaged or controlled by anyone's thoughts or feelings (including my own). I was not going to give Satan any selfish glory toward my detriment! *No, not today, Satan,* and every tomorrow is off-limits too!

I purposely did not go into significant (step-by-step) detail about the specifics of all I went through personally inside the church. Out of love, I did not disclose the names of those who deceived me, disappointed me, rejected me, or criticized me. I will not openly shame those who built a false witness against me because that is not the point of this message or this book (it is all under the blood). I decided to overcome and become a more Godlike Christian toward them, regardless of how they acted toward me. I have forgiven them, I love them, I pray for them, and I have chosen to rise above and soar like an eagle, because I am now qualified in the Spirit.

They have helped me, they are helping me, and those like them will help me to get to where Christ would have me yesterday, today, and forever! They taught me to watch my steps and allow God to order them as He called me on the path of righteousness for His namesake.

I can freely thank the Lord for the dirt, the mud, and the hard rocks that were thrown. The dirt helped to mold me, the mud made me a vessel for the Kingdom, and the rocks helped build and strengthen me in Christ. I sincerely thank God for the obstacles and the ministry traps that a few of my church brothers and sister set before me as they sought my spiritual demise. Now, just as Joseph could say to his brothers after they threw him in a pit to die, I can joyfully say as Joseph said, ***"Do not be afraid, for am I in the place of God? But as for you, you meant evil*** *against me; but God meant it for good, to bring it about as it is this day, to save many people alive"* (Gen. 50:19–20). The word of God remains a lamp to my feet and a light on my pathway of faith and in my progress of sanctification and fruit-filled growth. (Ps.119:105, 2 Tim. 2:21, 1 Thess. 5:23, Gal. 2:20, 2 Thess. 2:13).

I thank God for all my past, present, and future enemies if you want to know the truth! I have prayed more, fasted more, cried more, learned more, and I have grown more, all because the opposition pushed, pressed, and promoted me into my ministry! I have been liberated not just to overcome but to be a consistent overcomer! I have come over to the abundant life that Christ has promised you and me (John 10:10).

My being thankful to the Holy Spirit for my maturing and teaching me does not mean that what they did was not a horrible thing (or that I would desire to go through it all over again, because I would not). It does mean that I made the right choice to join my Savior and focus on His love and perfect will for my life. I chose to be a part of the remnant that God is building and raising to keep the standard, show forth Christ, promote His love, and carry His divine will in the Spirit of Kingdom excellence while being a blessing on this planet called Earth.

Healed

Glory to God! Now I can sincerely say, "I am totally healed!" I am open to hearing from the Spirit of God. I am willing to do whatever He would have me do, say, or pray concerning those who caused me pain, without fear or reservation.

The healing process was not easy; the pain was real, the tears were plentiful, and the hurt ran deep. But it was necessary for me that I may achieve the *divine goal* of growth, maturity, and freedom in Christ as an everlasting testimony of the grace afforded to me by God through

His only Son. If I want to succeed in things of God, I must trust Him. I now strive to be where He wants me to be daily, irrespective of the cost.

> *"No, dear brothers and sisters, I have not achieved it, but I focus on this one thing: Forgetting the past and looking forward to what lies ahead, I press on to reach the heavenly the prize for which God, through Christ Jesus is calling us. Let all who are spiritually mature agree on these things. If you disagree on some point, I believe God will make it plain to you."* (Phil. 3:13–15)

Did you read what that passage said, *"forgetting the past and looking forward to what lies ahead"*? Can you do that? Yes, you can because you are more aware now, and you desire to be spiritually mature! Our good Father has us covered, even during seasons of despair! He has made adequate provision for us not just to be free, but He has provided the power for us to stay free!

I had been appointed, anointed, ordained, called, and chosen by God Almighty (Elohim) to help and strengthen others in the things of God. I was assigned to teach, preach, speak, minister, and write books that would allow the Body of Christ to be better living illustrations of Christlike epistles (2 Cor. 3:1–6). I discovered that I was not going through what I was going through just for me. I am here to help admonish the Church to come back to the unadulterated and straightforward (yet powerful and effective) ways of Christ, and once again **be the Church**, *the called-out ones*, those who adhere to and follow the word, the works, and obey will of God. We are to represent and demonstrate Christ above all else; regardless of what others do (or do not do), we must exemplify Christ at any cost.

Due to my church hurt experience, I now know that it is okay to be loving, caring, different, unique, free, separated, consecrated, and, most times, isolated by God. It is for the process of sanctification, holy works, empowerment, and the abundance of all good things for my life, my good, the good of others, and ultimately for His glory. I refuse to leave or quit on God again. He did not bail on me in my darkest hours. He has never left or quit on me, and He never will. He's been faithful (Heb. 13:5, Deut. 31:6-8, Jos. 1:5-9).

Afterward, I was to apply it, begin to live it, teach it, write about it, and love it without compromise! This painful period was my pruning (cutting) and my growing season; it was the abyss of my journey to "here." I had to become extremely sensitive to the Spirit of God. I had to comply with the word quickly and follow His leading without doubting.

Just as the Spirit of God led me to discover things about myself that prompted me to do better, He will do the same for you. As He developed me in the spirit realm and taught me how to supernaturally get through the healing process of learning to forgive, love, move forward, and forget the trauma of church hurt, He will surely help you too. I do not doubt it!

Yes, those people tried to cross me out, then the devil wanted to cross me out, then I felt abandoned at the crossroads of life, but it was understanding the significance of the death-defying work of Christ on the Cross that brought me out!

What He did for me He can surely do for you! The following books in this series will help you more on your Christian journey, especially in ministry. Would you please read them with an open heart and allow the Holy Spirit of God to lead you into true Christianity and *overcome* church hurt?

Get Up!

I hope by now you somewhat get the point of what salvation should do to someone who indeed has given their life to Christ without reservation. If you have not yet had this experience in some way, ask yourself why. Honestly pray and ask God why you haven't had a life-altering encounter with Christ after being hurt. Wholeheartedly seek the scriptures for His answer to your questions. You may also need to ask your pastor, ministry leader, or a wise Saint to help you and give you some wisdom for your journey.

Here are some scriptures that may help you (ESV):

Matthew 6:33:
> *"But seek first the kingdom of God and his righteousness, and all these things will be added to you."*

Hebrews 11:6:
> *"And without faith it is impossible to please him, for whoever would draw near to God must believe that he exists and that he rewards those who seek him."*

1 Chronicles 16:11:
  "Seek the Lord and his strength; seek his presence continually!"

Proverbs 8:17:
  "I love those who love me, and those who seek me diligently find me."

Jeremiah 29:13:
  "You will seek me and find me, when you seek me with all your heart."

Psalm 63:1:
  "O God, you are my God; earnestly I seek you; my soul thirsts for you; my flesh faints for you, as in a dry and weary land where there is no water."

Matthew 7:7–8:
  "Ask, and it will be given to you; seek, and you will find; knock, and it will be opened to you. For everyone who asks receives, and the one who seeks finds, and to the one who knocks it will be opened."

Psalm 9:10:
  "And those who know your name put their trust in you, for you, O Lord, have not forsaken those who seek you."

Psalm 14:2:
  "The Lord looks down from heaven on the children of man, to see if there are any who understand, who seek after God."

Psalm 34:10:
  "The young lions suffer want and hunger; but those who seek the Lord lack no good thing."

Isaiah 55:6–7:
"Seek the Lord while he may be found; call upon him while he is near; let the wicked forsake his way, and the unrighteous man his thoughts; let him return to the Lord, that he may have compassion on him, and to our God, for he will abundantly pardon."

Psalm 119:2:
"Blessed are those who keep his testimonies, who seek him with their whole heart."

Psalm 119:10:
"With my whole heart I seek you; let me not wander from your commandments!"

Lamentations 3:25:
"The Lord is good to those who wait for him, to the soul who seeks him."

2 Chronicles 7:14:
"If my people who are called by my name humble themselves, and pray and seek my face and turn from their wicked ways, then I will hear from heaven and will forgive their sin and heal their land."

James 4:8:
"Draw near to God, and he will draw near to you. Cleanse your hands, you sinners, and purify your hearts, you double-minded."

Matthew 7:7:
"Ask, and it will be given to you; seek, and you will find; knock, and it will be opened to you."

Psalm 105:4:
> *"Seek the Lord and his strength; seek his presence continually!"*

Psalm 40:16:
> *"But may all who seek you rejoice and be glad in you; may those who love your salvation say continually, 'Great is the Lord!'"*

Acts 17:27:
> *"That they should seek God, in the hope that they might feel their way toward him and find him. Yet he is actually not far from each one of us."*

I encourage you to read the entire New Testament (especially John, Acts, Romans, Corinthians, Ephesians, Galatians, and James), as you will discover that double-minded, opinionated, casual, comfortable, and convenient Christianity should be unacceptable to any authentic Christ-follower.

Do Not Ignore the Truth

Far too many people are claiming Christianity, but they are not genuine Christ-followers. They do not represent God very well (if at all). They are hurting others in a worse way. They mock Christianity in their lifestyles, words, and actions that do not line up with the scriptures. They justify it all by misusing, misinterpreting, and misunderstanding the scriptures to suit their lusts and other sinful desires.

These spiritual injustices and grievances can plague the minds of believers and nonbelievers alike for years if not correctly dealt with on an individual basis. Experiences such as these often-attenuate people's faith, hope, and confidence in God (especially young/new believers). Church hurt has turned far too many people away from uniting with specific fellowships of believers. The things mentioned can weigh heavily on vulnerable hearts and fragile minds, as they are unacceptable and extremely destructive in so many ways.

Christian vs Form of Godliness

Let us look closely at the type of people I am referring to according to 2 Timothy 3.

> *"But understand this, that in the last days there will come times of difficulty. For people will be lovers of self, lovers of money, proud, arrogant, abusive, disobedient to their parents, ungrateful, unholy, heartless, unappeasable, slanderous, without self-control, brutal, not loving good, treacherous, reckless, swollen with conceit, lovers of pleasure rather than lovers of God, having the appearance of godliness but denying its power. Avoid such people."* (2 Tim. 3:1–5)

Paul describes the nature of the people in the last days (and these are indeed the last days). He warns us about some Christian believers who seem to have an "appearance (form) of godliness but denying its power." Then he says, "avoid (stay away) from these people." Other versions of this scripture say, "Have nothing to do with such people," so why would an Apostle, a holy man of God, a disciple of the Holy Spirit utter such harsh words?

His words are to provoke thought or conversation and are also to be highly evaluated by those genuinely claiming Christ. There should be solid and ongoing evidence of God in the lives of every believer! This evidence should complement the proper form of godliness since the Holy Spirit lives in, transforms, and leads the lives of real Christ-followers. He uncompromisingly leads believers into a lifestyle of holiness, righteousness, and godly love (1 Cor. 6:19). The indwelling of the Holy Spirit will lead every believer into Christlike behavior (if they allow Him). He empowers the believer to bear good fruit.

The fruit (attributes) of having the Holy Spirit is love, joy, peace, patience, kindness, goodness, faithfulness, gentleness, and self-control, and there is no natural or spiritual law against being (not pretending to be) those things (Gal. 5:22–23). These are attributes of a faithful Christian, and they are the antithesis of what the Apostle Paul lists as sins in 2 Timothy 3:1–4. Godly fruit does not lie, deceive, backbite, gossip, hate, fornicate, manipulate, steal, or practice sin or any ungodly and wicked acts mentioned in the word of God.

Christians cannot present themselves as children of God if there is no godly fruit, no clear evidence of power, or permanent lifestyle change. You are not a legitimate Christ-follower because you dress up in costly sparkling attire, display religious garb, and sit in lofty seats. Orating and pontificating prolifically, studying Hebrew, Greek, *Christianese*, and knowing the scriptures from Genesis to Revelations doesn't make you a true child of God. Having spiritual gifts, casting out devils, and speaking in an unknown tongue doesn't mean you are loving and forgiving; it means you were in right standing with God when you received the gift.

"For God's gifts and His call are irrevocable. [He never withdraws them when once they are given, and He does not change His mind about those to whom He gives His grace or to whom He sends His call]" (Rom. 11:29, AMP).

If you are not striving to honor Christ wholeheartedly in your daily walk (actions), talk, thoughts, and overall lifestyle, then you are a fake. False Christians are detrimental and destructive to the ministry of the Gospel of Christ. Identify yourself in the scriptures!

James identifies true faith (James 2:14–26). True faith (the evidence of what you believe is to come according to the word of God) adheres to hope under any circumstance and above every obstacle. True faith does not make excuses for not standing for Christ (Eph. 6:13).

Church folks professing Christianity with no active evidence of faith do not bear good fruit; you must guard your heart against them and avoid their contamination! They are not honoring God and only display an outward appearance of godliness. Yet their words, actions, and compassion are far from Him (study what Christ said to the pretentious religious people in Matthew 15:1–20). Yes, keep these people far from you (pray diligently for their souls, but do not trust them), or they will grievously hurt you in some shape, form, or way!

As Christians, faith alone (standing alone and not accompanied by godly actions) is dead (James 2:17, 26). Your trust must demonstrate total confidence in God; there is no other way. You are deceiving yourselves if you think you can be spiritual, live a holy life, and be effective Christ-followers by only hearing the Word. Hearing and doing are not the same, just as knowing and doing are not the same. So what good is your faith if there are no real actions to justify your belief? Are you glorifying Christ in your walk, talk, and thoughts? Where is the life of Christ-life seen in you? What good fruit of your holy, sanctified, and reformed lifestyle producing for others to see and glean (John 15:8)?

The fruit of the Spirit is love, joy, peace, patience, kindness, goodness, faithfulness, gentleness, and self-control (Gal. 5:22–23). This fruit should be the main characteristic of a faithful Christian follower. This fruit is a description of Christlike behavior, and it all stems from love. If you do not have real love, no actual Christlike fruit will be genuinely displayed through you! Christian behavior involves not only receiving Christ but also being more like Christ in every way. Being fruit-filled and fruitful is indicated in how we treat others. Being a witness to God's love through Christ shows when we tell others but more so when we live it out when we share the Gospel with others (read the book of Romans). You must continually accentuate God's love and compassion for the lost as demonstrated by Christ (He provides the most excellent example of what Christian behavior should look like daily). **Does your behavior line up with the word and the will of God?**

Get Up!

The Holy Spirit led me on a journey within a journey, an experience within an experience, to get me where I needed to be in Him. I had to put Christ back in His rightful place in my life as Lord. I had to get out of the pit!

I was compelled to write what I am writing to help individuals in the body of Christ (all members, all races, all sects, all groups, denominations, and non-denominations). I was unsuspectingly caught in one of many "ministry traps" set by the devil for believers.

I was in the wrong place, and I had the church in the wrong place in my heart. I had too many expectations of the people. I wanted from them what only God could provide. I felt abandoned and "crossed out" by the church, but the church was where I needed to be the most.

Due to my church hurt experience, I now know that it is okay to be loving, caring, different, unique, free, separated, consecrated and, most times, isolated by God. It was necessary for the process of sanctification, holy works, empowerment, and the abundance of all good things for my life, my good, the good of others, and ultimately for His glory. I refuse to leave or quit on God again. He did not bail on me in mu darkest hours. He has never left me or quit on me, and He never will. He's been faithful (Heb. 13:5, Deut. 31:6-8, Jos. 1:5-9). I realized that one day is a day too long to harbor unforgiveness in any way toward anyone. I allowed my flesh to keep me from the God that genuinely loved me and who held my recovery in His word and His nail-imprinted hands.

Once spiritual revelation and reformation began, I *slowly* started walking back into the things of God. I had a calling to fulfill my divine destiny in Christ (believe me, it was one of the most challenging choices I have ever had to make). There was still work for me to do, but I had to get up! I enjoyed the Christ-life, and up to a point, I enjoyed going to church! How could I let the enemy win so easily?

After many tears, much seclusion, ongoing prayer, and revelation, it was time to get up! I discovered that I had to push beyond the past and allow the Holy Spirit to convert my pain into power and move beyond the pain (Eph. 3:20). I understood that I had a *"faith mission possible"* to complete despite the impossibilities placed in my path.

For months I allowed my flesh to keep me from the God that genuinely loved me and held my recovery in His word and His hands. I should have heeded the scripture and thought on God's perfect will and plan for my life, not what "they" did or said to me. I eventually apprehended that one day is a day too long to harbor unforgiveness in any way toward anyone.

I had to go all out, give it all up, start all over again with Christ, and walk into a place of true discipleship despite the agony. Amid the excruciating aches and desolation, I still wanted to be a virtuous Christian, a respectable woman of God, and a triumphant success in Kingdom building. I had to become adequately qualified to disregard the pain and not rehearse my woes to become those things. My difficulty was ignoring pain while discovering the spiritual ethics of authentic ministry looked like through Christ, according to His word concerning all Christians.

Then I was to apply it, live it, teach it, write about it, and love it without compromise! This painful period was my pruning (cutting) and my growing season; it was the abyss of my journey to "here." I had to become overly sensitive to the Spirit of God in such a way to cause me to comply without doubting quickly.

I realized that faith without a test was just idle talk. Faith without trials cannot be proven. It can only be used when a force directly or indirectly opposes its ability to get results. Faith has no real strength when it is dormant; it shows its true nature and power during the testing. In other words, you do not know if something works until it has been tried and proven to work (read James chapter 1). Getting up was one task, but standing and staying up during persecution would be another task of faith, which requires total reliance upon God (Heb. chapter 11).

From the first day I encountered the living God, my life changed when I put my total trust in Him! When I served, I served with all my heart! When I prayed, I prayed in faith! I said "Yes, Lord," and surrendered my life to Him, and it was for a lifetime! I was a genuine, faithful believer and a committed Christ-follower. I was utterly sold-out to the Lord Jesus Christ. I once again chose (and was chosen) to fight the good fight of faith and not sit in ignorance but to get up in strength and wisdom! I decided to be different and chose a better path. I did not desire to *fit in* anymore; I wanted to stand out on purpose, because I was called out with a purpose. I decided to live a holy, sanctified, and set-apart life, to do Kingdom ministry without compromise. I decided to be a red-hot Christ-follower for the glory of God. I decided to *get up* for Him, to help you and to help them!

We, as Christians, cannot walk by faith unless we **get up in faith and rise up in victory**! I pray, trust, believe, and decree that no demonic spirit using the actions of people will ever stop us again! After all we've been through, we will not let Satan keep taking our love, joy, or peace anymore! We will live by faith as we victoriously fight the "good" fight of faith in Christ. We refuse to lose! We are practicing winners, not practicing sinners! Our God is on our side, we are more than conquerors, we will spread the Gospel, and we will do successful Kingdom ministry in the name of Jesus! We will compel souls to come by the leading of

God's Spirit. We win because Christ won! We will not be a defeated people; we will arise in the glory and power of the Lord!

In the name of Jesus, get up, get up, get up!

CPSIA information can be obtained
at www.ICGtesting.com
Printed in the USA
LVHW080340020422
715079LV00003B/3